TALK TO ME IN KOREAN
LEVEL 8

Improve Proficiency with Idiomatic Phrases, Tense Structures, and Situational Expressions

This book is based on a series of published lessons, divided into ten levels, which are currently available at TalkToMeInKorean.com.

TALK TO ME IN KOREAN
- LEVEL 8 -

Talk To Me In Korean - Level 8

| 1판 1쇄 | 1st edition published | 2020. 5. 4 |
| 1판 2쇄 | 2nd edition published | 2020. 7. 14 |

지은이	Written by	TalkToMeInKorean
책임편집	Edited by	선경화 Kyung-hwa Sun, 에밀리 프리즈러키 Emily Przylucki
디자인	Designed by	선윤아 Yoona Sun
삽화	Illustrations by	김경해 Kyounghae Kim
녹음	Voice Recordings by	선현우 Hyunwoo Sun, 최경은 Kyeong-eun Choi
펴낸곳	Published by	롱테일북스 Longtail Books
펴낸이	Publisher	이수영 Su Young Lee
편집	Copy-edited by	김보경 Florence Kim
주소	Address	04043 서울 마포구 양화로 12길 16-9(서교동) 북앤빌딩 3층
		3rd Floor Book-And Bldg. 16-9 Yanghwa-ro 12-gil, Mapo-gu, Seoul, KOREA
이메일	E-mail	TTMIK@longtailbooks.co.kr
ISBN		979-11-86701-99-7 14710

이 도서의 국립중앙도서관 출판예정도서목록(CIP)은 서지정보유통지원시스템 홈페이지(http://seoji.nl.go.kr)와
국가자료종합목록 구축시스템(https://kolis-net.nl.go.kr)에서 이용하실 수 있습니다.
(CIP제어번호 : CIP2020014746)

TTMIK - TALK TO ME IN KOREAN

MESSAGE
FROM
THE AUTHOR

You have come a long way! At this point, learning Korean is probably a very natural part of your daily life. Having reached Level 8 of the Talk To Me In Korean curriculum means that you did not stop learning when you felt like you already knew enough. It means that you have stayed motivated even when there were other distractions and temptations.

We make our lessons bite-sized and relatively short in order to make sure that you are not overwhelmed, but that doesn't mean it is an easy thing to finish an entire book, let alone 7 different levels! Now that you are at Level 8, you are ready more than ever to take your Korean to the next level so that you can really incorporate it not only into your daily life, but also into your work life and future endeavors. You will start seeing more opportunities as you speak Korean even more fluently and accurately. You will naturally make more connections with people because you have a good knowledge of the language. We hope you keep on learning, not just out of necessity but as part of your lifestyle.

벌써 레벨 8까지 오신 걸 축하드리고, 저희 책으로 공부해 주셔서 감사합니다! 앞으로도 계속 즐겁게 공부하실 수 있을 거라고 믿어요. 저희 톡투미 인 코리안 팀 모두, 한국어 학습자 여러분들을 응원하고 있을게요!

TABLE OF
CONTENTS

LESSON **1**

Advanced Idiomatic Expressions I (Part I)

눈 (Eye)

Track 01

Welcome to the first lesson in the Advanced Idiomatic Expression series! By studying with this series, you will learn many idiomatic expressions that are based on a certain Korean word and used in everyday Korean conversation. In order to fully understand and use the expressions introduced in this series, it is essential that you understand the grammatical structure of the sentence. When you come across a grammar point with which you are unfamiliar, please go back and review the related lessons.

Keyword: 눈 = eye

Part I

I. 눈이 높다 = to be picky

  ▷ 높다 = to be high; to have high standards

  ▷ Synonym: 까다롭다

눈이 높다 literally means that your "eyes are high", but in Korean, if you say that your eyes are 높다, it simply means that you have high standards for things or people. When someone is very picky about the type of person they want to date or the kind of things they want to buy, you can say 눈이 높다.

Ex)

저 눈 안 높아요. 저는 그냥 성격 좋은 사람이면 다 좋아요.

= I am not picky. Anyone who has a good personality is fine for me.

2. **눈 밖에 나다** = to get on one's bad side

▷ 밖에 = outside of something

▷ 나다 = to get out; to be out

If you did something to make someone upset with you, and that person does not like you very much any longer, you may end up on their bad side.

In that case, you can say that you are "outside" someone's eyes, meaning that the person will not help you or give you any support.

This expression is not usually used amongst friends; it is typically used by adults like teachers or bosses to students or employees.

Ex)

저는 지각을 많이 해서, 선생님 눈 밖에 났어요.

= I am frequently late, so my teacher does not like me [I got on my teacher's bad side].

3. 눈을 붙이다 = to get some sleep; to take a nap

   ▷ 붙이다 = to paste; to glue things together

When you take a nap, you can use the expression 눈을 붙이다. The literal translation is "to glue one's eyes together", but it is actually closer in meaning to "gluing one's eyelids shut", meaning that one naps or sleeps. This phrase is not commonly used for sleeping at night.

Ex)

피곤하면 눈 좀 붙여요. 나중에 깨워 줄게요.

= If you are tired, get some sleep. I will wake you up later.

You can even say, "눈 좀 붙이고 올게요. (= I will go catch some sleep.)"

Track 01

4. 눈빛만 봐도 알 수 있다 = can know with just one glance

   ▷ 빛 = light

   ▷ 보다 = to see

   ▷ 알다 = to know

   ▷ 만 = only

When you automatically know what a person wants or wishes to tell you just by looking at them, you can say 눈빛만 봐도 알 수 있다. The word 눈빛 does not literally refer to light that comes out of one's eyes, but rather the way someone looks at something or the emotion that you can sense from looking at their eyes.

Ex)

말 안 해도, 눈빛만 봐도 알 수 있어요.

= Even if you do not say it, I know just by looking at your eyes.

5. **눈앞이 캄캄하다** = to not know where to start; to have no hope

▷ 앞 = front

▷ 캄캄하다 = to be dark; to be pitch black

Ex)

불을 끄면 캄캄해져요.

= If you turn off the lights, it will be dark.

When it is dark, you might panic because you cannot see anything in front of you. When you are confronted with a situation where you do not know what to do or you cannot think of a way to get out of it, you can say 눈앞이 캄캄하다.

Ex)

눈앞이 캄캄했었는데, 석진 씨가 도와줬어요.

= I panicked because I did not know how to solve the problem, but then 석진 helped me.

Track 01

6. **눈썰미가 좋다** = to learn things quickly; to pick things up quickly

▷ 좋다 = to be good

눈썰미 refers to the ability to learn or understand how something is done just by watching someone else doing it. For example, when someone learns how to cook a Korean dish mainly by watching others, or when someone picks up a dance move very quickly by imitating what they saw, you can say that the person has good 눈썰미.

Ex)

한 번만 보고 어떻게 따라해요? 눈썰미가 좋으시네요!

= How do you follow the moves just by looking at them once? You pick up things very quickly!

11

센스가 있다 has a similar meaning but it is a bit broader. If you are quick to figure out what to do or have an innate sense or feel for something, people will say 센스가 있다.

Track 01

Sample Dialogue

경은: 도와줘서 고마워. 혼자 하려고
하니까 눈앞이 캄캄했어.

현우: 아니야. 이걸 어떻게 혼자 해. 혼자
다 못 하지.

경은: 일하다가 피곤하면 저기서 눈 좀
붙여. 알겠지?

현우: 응, 알겠어. 우리 조금만 더 힘내자!

Kyeong-eun: *Thanks for helping me. I was trying to do it
by myself but I panicked.*

Hyunwoo: *No worries. It's impossible for you to do this
all by yourself. You can't finish this on your
own.*

Kyeong-eun: *If you get tired while working on it, get
some sleep over there. Okay?*

Hyunwoo: *Okay. Let's keep going.*

13

✏ Exercises for Lesson 1

Fill in the blanks with the appropriate idioms with 는 from the lesson.

1. (   )

    = can know with just one glance

2. (   )

    = to not know where to start; to have no hope

3. (   )

    = to get some sleep; to take a nap

4. (   )

    = to get on one's bad side

5. (   )

    = to learn things quickly; to pick things up quickly

Check the answers on **p. 207**

LESSON **2**

Advanced Idiomatic Expressions 1 (Part 2)

눈 (Eye)

This is Part 2 of the Advanced Idiomatic Expressions lessons related to 눈, the eyes! In order to fully understand and use the expressions introduced in this series, it is essential that you understand the grammatical structure of the sentence. When you come across a grammar point with which you are unfamiliar, please go back and review the related lessons.

Track
03

Keyword: 눈 = eye

In Part 1, you learned the following expressions: (See Level 8 Lesson 1)

1. 눈이 높다 = to be picky

2. 눈 밖에 나다 = to get on one's bad side

3. 눈을 붙이다 = to get some sleep; to take a nap

4. 눈빛만 봐도 알 수 있다 = can know with just one glance

5. 눈앞이 캄캄하다 = to not know where to start; to have no hope

6. 눈썰미가 좋다 = to learn things quickly; to pick things up quickly

Part 2

7. 눈에 넣어도 아프지 않다 = to be the apple of one's eye

▷ 넣다 = to put in

▷ 아프다 = to hurt

▷ 아프지 않다 = to not hurt

Track 03

눈에 넣다 literally means "to put something into one's eyes", like eye drops. However, here it is part of 눈에 넣어도 아프지 않다, which literally means, "Someone is so precious that it will not hurt even if you put him/her into your eyes." It might be a bit strange to think about the literal meaning of this sentence, so think of it more as "being the apple of one's eye / not hurting to look at someone". This is usually used toward children or when talking about someone you think is attractive.

Ex)

아이들은 그 나이 때 정말 귀여워서 눈에 넣어도 아프지 않아요.

= Kids at that age are so cute that they are the apple of your eye.

8. 눈에 띄다 = to be difficult to miss; to stand out

▷ 띄다 = to be spotted

The verb 띄다 itself means to be spotted, but it is almost always used with the noun 눈 to form the phrase 눈에 띄다. When you say that something or someone is 눈에 띄다, it not only means that it catches your eye and is remarkable, but it can also mean that something is difficult to miss because it is either very good or terrible. When someone's fashion stands out because it is either amazing or weird, you can say 눈에 띄는 패션, and when someone's

16

Korean speaking skills have improved a lot, you can say that the person's Korean has, "눈에 띄게 늘었어요."

Ex)

한국어 어떻게 공부해요? 실력이 눈에 띄게 늘었어요!

= How do you study Korean? Your Korean skills have improved so much!

경은 씨는 눈에 띄게 예쁜 사람이에요.

= Kyeong-eun is an outstandingly beautiful person.

9. 눈을 마주치다 = eyes meet

▷ 마주치다 = to run into each other; to bump into each other

▷ 치다 = to hit someone

Track 03

마주치다 means "to bump into" or "to run into someone" by chance. When you use this verb with 눈, it means that two people's eyes meet. When you say 눈을 마주치다, 눈 is the object of the verb 마주치다; you can also say 눈이 마주치다, with 눈 as the subject of the verb 마주치다.

Ex)

둘이 눈을 마주치고 웃었어요.

= The two people's eyes met and they smiled.

그 사람하고 눈이 마주쳤는데, 창피해서 고개를 돌렸어요.

= My eyes met his, and I felt embarrassed so I looked away.

10. 눈이 멀다 = to be blinded by something

▷ 눈이 멀다 = to go blind

17

Here, the verb 멀다 sounds the same as the verb for "to be far away", but when 멀다 is used with 눈, it means that your eyes are temporarily blinded by something. This expression is often used with the thing that caused you to be blinded in the form of "Noun + -에 눈이 멀다".

Ex)
그 사람은 욕심에 눈이 멀었어요.
= He is blinded by his greed.

This phrase could mean to go blind, but there are other, more common expressions for that.

Track 03

Ex)
시력을 잃다 = to lose one's eyesight
눈이 안 보이다 = to not be able to see

II. **눈이 부시다** = to be radiant
  ▷ 눈이 부시다 = to be dazzling; to be too bright

눈이 부시다 means that something is so bright that you cannot open your eyes to look at it directly. You can use this expression to talk about light, but you can also say this about someone's looks.

Ex)
눈이 부시게 아름다워요.
= Your beauty is dazzling.

12. **눈 하나 깜짝하지 않다** = to not bat an eye
  ▷ 하나 = one
  ▷ 깜짝하다 = to blink

When someone is not surprised or affected by a threatening or shocking remark or action, you can say that the person does not even blink at it. You can use the expression 눈 하나 깜짝하지 않다, or 눈 하나 깜짝 안 하다.

Ex)

그 사람은 그런 말을 들어도 눈 하나 깜짝하지 않을 거예요.

= Even if you tell him that, he would not bat an eye.

A similar expression is 눈 깜짝할 사이에, which means "in the blink of an eye".
  ▷ 사이 = a period of time

Track 03

Ex)

눈 깜짝할 사이에 일을 다 끝냈어요.

= In the blink of an eye, they finished all the work.

* When Koreans actually want to say "to blink", they use the expression 깜빡이다 rather than 깜짝하다.

19

Sample Dialogue

현우: 예지 씨 조카들은 너무 귀여워서 눈에 넣어도 아프지 않을 것 같아요!

예지: 네, 맞아요! 저를 보고 방긋방긋 웃을 때가 제일 사랑스러워요.

현우: 정말요? 저희 조카들은 저랑 눈만 마주치면 울어요.

예지: 현우 씨가 항상 괴롭히니까 울 수밖에 없죠!

Hyunwoo: *Your nieces/nephews are so adorable. They must be the apple of your eye.*

Yeji: *Exactly! They are cutest when they smile at me.*

Hyunwoo: *Really? My nieces/nephews burst into tears whenever our eyes meet.*

Yeji: *Of course they cry. You always bug them!*

✎ Exercises for Lesson 2

Fill in the blanks with the appropriate idioms with 눈 from the lesson.

1. (   )

= to not bat an eye

2. (   )

= to be the apple of one's eye

3. (   )

= to be blinded by something

4. (   )

= to be radiant

5. (   )

= to be difficult to miss; to stand out

Check the answers on **p. 207**

LESSON **3**

Right after -ing

-기가 무섭게, -기가 바쁘게

**Track
05**

We have already introduced how to say "as soon as" or "right after" in Korean in Level 5, Lesson 7, but there is more than one way to say these phrases in Korean. In this lesson, we will introduce a more advanced and figurative way of saying "as soon as".

I. Verb + -기가 무섭게

The word 무섭다 literally means "to be scary" or "to be scared", but -기가 무섭게 has nothing to do with being scared or scary in its translation. When you say that something happens right after you do something, or even "as" you are doing it, you can say "Verb + -기가 무섭게" and then say what happened.

Ex)
수업이 끝나기가 무섭게 = as soon as the class ended; as the class was finishing
= 수업이 끝나자마자

* You are really emphasizing just how fast everyone left or did something after the class finished.

말이 끝나기가 무섭게 = as soon as he finished talking
= 말이 끝나자마자

2. Verb + -기가 바쁘게

-기가 바쁘게 and -기가 무섭게 are almost always interchangeable and are used depending on personal preference. However, in everyday conversations, -기가 바쁘게 is used less commonly than -기가 무섭게 in general.

Track
05

Ex)
문을 열기가 바쁘게 = as soon as I opened the doors
= 문을 열자마자

밥을 다 먹기가 바쁘게 = as soon as he finished eating
= 밥을 다 먹자마자

Please note that you do not usually use -기가 무섭게 and -기가 바쁘게 in imperative sentences or in "Let us" sentences. They are usually used in the past tense or the present tense.

Sample Sentences
아침에 눈을 뜨기가 무섭게 집에서 나왔어요.

23

= 아침에 눈을 뜨기가 바쁘게 집에서 나왔어요.

= As soon as I woke up in the morning, I left the house.

문을 열기가 무섭게 손님들이 들어왔어요.

= 문을 열기가 바쁘게 손님들이 들어왔어요.

= As soon as we opened the door, customers came in.

음식이 주문하기가 무섭게 나왔어요.

= 음식이 주문하기가 바쁘게 나왔어요.

= The food came out as soon as we ordered it.

수업이 끝나기가 무섭게 학생들이 교실 밖으로 나갔어요.

= 수업이 끝나기가 바쁘게 학생들이 교실 밖으로 나갔어요.

= The students left the classroom as soon as the class was over.

사람들은 공연이 끝나기가 무섭게 밖으로 나갔어요.

= 사람들은 공연이 끝나기가 바쁘게 밖으로 나갔어요.

= As soon as the performance was over, people went outside.

Sample Dialogue

Track 06

경은: 주연 씨 어디 갔어요?

석진: 일 끝나기가 무섭게 집에 갔어요.

경은: 아, 벌써요?

석진: 네. 친구 만난다고 6시 되기가
　　　무섭게 퇴근했어요.

Kyeong-eun: Where is Jooyeon?

Seokjin: She headed home as soon as she got her
　　　work done.

Kyeong-eun: Did she? Already?

Seokjin: Yes. As soon as it turned 6, she got off work
　　　to meet her friend.

✏ *Exercises for Lesson* **3**

Fill in the blanks using -**기가 무섭게** *or* -**기가 바쁘게**.

1. 현우 씨는 (   ) 바닥에 누웠어요.

    = As soon as he finished eating, Hyunwoo lay down on the floor.

2. 사람들은 (   ) 밖으로 나갔어요.

    = As soon as the performance was over, people went outside.

3. (   ) 개들이 짖기 시작했어요.

    = As soon as I opened the door, the dogs started barking.

4. (   ) 학생들이 교실 밖으로 나갔어요.

    = The students left the classroom as soon as the class was over.

5. 음식이 (   ) 나왔어요.

    = The food came out as soon as we ordered it.

Check the answers on **p. 207**

LESSON **4**

Noun + that (someone) used to + verb

-(았/었/였)던

You have already learned several ways to express past actions in Korean, such as using the -았/었/였어요 sentence ending for plain past tense sentences and -(으)ㄴ verb ending to modify a noun with an action verb. In this lesson, we will introduce something that is similar to -(으)ㄴ, but a little bit different.

Track
07

-던 = Noun + that (someone) used to + Verb

When you add -던 at the end of a verb stem, it expresses that you "used to" do or be something. The difference between -(으)ㄴ and -던 is that -던 implies that the past action or state did not continue or has been completed.

For example, with the verb 가다 (= to go), if you say 간 곳, it means a place that "you went to" in the past, but if you say 가던 곳, it means that "you used to go there" but somehow, the act of going there came to an end and did not continue.

With the verb 보다 (= to see), if you say 본 영화, it means a movie that you "watched" before, but if you say 보던 영화, it implies that you did not finish it.

Ex)

어제 보던 영화

= a movie one was watching yesterday (but did not finish / did not continue to watch)

-던 and -았/었/였던

With action verbs, it is sufficient to just use -던, but you can make the meaning of the past tense stronger by adding -았/었/였. With descriptive verbs, it is almost always more natural to use -았/었/였던.

Track 07

Ex)

예쁘다 = to be pretty
→ 예쁘던 (less natural)
→ 예뻤던 (more natural)

작다 = to be small
→ 작던 (less natural)
→ 작았던 (more natural)

비싸다 = to be expensive
→ 비싸던 (less natural)
→ 비쌌던 (more natural)

So remember, if a state or an action that used to happen did not continue or came to an end and you are no longer doing it, you can use -던 or -았/었/였던.

Sample Sentences

예전에 제가 자주 가던 곳이에요.

= I used to frequently go to this place in the past.

= It is a place that I often used to go to before.

    * The person is not going there anymore or as often.

예뻤던 경은 씨가 지금은...

= Kyeong-eun, who used to be pretty, is now...

    * Since 예쁘다 is a descriptive verb, you must use 예뻤던, not 예쁘던.

Track
07

작년에는 키가 작았던 석진 씨가 지금은 키가 커요.

= Seokjin, who was short last year, is now tall.

    * 작은 (x), 작던 (x)

친했던 친구들이 지금은 다 외국에 살아요.

= The friends I used to be close to are all living overseas now.

    * 친한 (x), 친하던 (x)

지난주에 이야기하던 거예요.

= This is what we were talking about last week [but did not finish].

    * If you say, "지난주에 이야기한 거예요", it means, "This is what we talked about last week."

이거 누가 먹던 거예요?

= Who was eating this?

여기 있던 가게가 없어졌어요.

= The store that used to be here is gone.

여기 있던 핸드폰 못 봤어요?

= Haven't you seen the phone that was here?

Track 07

Sample Dialogue

Track 08

주연: 경화 씨, 이게 다 뭐예요?

경화: 예전에 입었던 옷이랑 신발인데 누구 주려고요.

주연: 이 신발도요? 이거 경화 씨가 정말 좋아했던 신발 아니에요?

경화: 맞아요. 근데 어차피 가지고 있어도 안 신을 것 같아요.

Jooyeon: Kyung-hwa, what are all these things?

Kyung-hwa: These are some clothes and shoes that I used to wear, but I am planning to give them away.

Jooyeon: Even these shoes? Aren't they ones that you used to like a lot?

Kyung-hwa: Right. But I think I am not going to wear them anymore anyway, even if I keep them.

✎ Exercises for Lesson 4

Fill in the boxes provided to match the English translation.

1. 제가 ☐☐ 책이에요.

= That is a book that I did not finish.

2. ☐☐☐ 친구들이 지금은 다 외국에 살아요.

= The friends I used to be close to are all living overseas now.

3. 작년에는 키가 ☐☐☐ 석진 씨가 지금은 키가 커요.

= Seokjin, who was short last year, is now tall.

Translate the sentences below into Korean and write them on the lines provided.

4. This is what we were talking about last week.

....

5. It is a place that I often used to go to before.

....

LESSON 5

Advanced Situational Expressions 1

거절할 때
(Refusing in Korean)

Welcome to the first lesson in the Advanced Situational Expressions series. Throughout this series, we will take a look at some common situations and some of the advanced expressions you can use in each of them. In this lesson, we will introduce various expressions you can use when you want to refuse or say no to something (you may think of 싫어요, which is a basic way to say no, but that is more for children).

Track 09

1.

괜찮아요. = It is okay (even if you do not offer it to me).

괜찮습니다. (same as above but more formal)

저는 괜찮습니다. = I am good. / I am okay. / I am fine without it.

* This is typically used in really formal situations or to people much older than you.

2.

아니에요. = No (you do not have to). / No (I do not need it).

아닙니다. (same as above but more formal)

* You can also say, "아니에요. 괜찮아요."

** You can use, "아니에요" or "아닙니다" to refuse something or to say, "I am flattered" to a comment.

3.

됐어요. = Do not worry about it. / I do not need that. / I am all set even without it.

됐습니다. (same as above but more formal)

* "됐어요" or "됐습니다" is a little more harsh than the expressions above. So, if you say this, it will sound like you are upset.

4.

생각이 없어요. = I am not hungry. / I am fine. / No thanks. (when offered food)

생각이 없습니다. (same as above but more formal)

* You can use this also if you have said no and they keep offering.

5.

안 그러셔도 괜찮아요. = You do not have to do that. / Please do not bother doing that.

안 그러셔도 괜찮습니다. (same as above but more formal)

6.

곤란해요. = It is difficult and embarrassing. / I cannot do it.

곤란합니다. (same as above but more formal)

지금은 좀 곤란합니다. = I cannot do it now.

이러시면 곤란합니다. = You should not do this. / You are making things difficult for me by doing this.

* Most of the time when you use this phrase, 지금은 is added.

7.

안 돼요. = No, I cannot. / No, you cannot. / It does not work. / It is not allowed.

안 됩니다. (same as above but more formal)

이러시면 안 됩니다. = You should not do this. / You can not do this.

안 될 것 같습니다. = I think this will be a problem. / I think you should not do it.

8.

이러지 마세요. = Do not do this.

* Typically you use this when you are really upset.

9.

어려울 것 같습니다. = I do not think I can do it. / I think it will be difficult. / I think it will be impossible.

* If someone says this, take it as a "no".

Track
09

Sample Dialogue

Track
10

진우: 수진 씨, 저희랑 같이 점심 먹을래요?

수진: 아, 저는 괜찮습니다. 드시고 오세요.

진우: 점심 약속 있어요?

수진: 아, 아니요. 그냥 지금은 밥 생각이
　　　없어서요.

Jinwoo: Sujin, do you want to have lunch with us?

Sujin: Ah, I am good. Enjoy your lunch.

Jinwoo: Do you have other plans for lunch?

Sujin: Ah, no, I am just not in the mood.

✏ Exercises for Lesson *5*

How would you respond to your coworker in each situation? Write it down in Korean using the phrases from the lesson.

1. Your coworker asks if you want some cookies, but you are too stuffed to take them.

....

2. It is lunchtime. Your coworker asked if you want her to buy your lunch while she is at it, but you think she does not have to.

....

3. Your coworker asks if you can do him a favor, but you are too busy at the moment.

....

4. Your coworker keeps apologizing to you because of a mistake that he made, but you are too upset to forgive him.

....

5. Your coworker's insistence has gotten to a point where you find it unacceptable.

....

Check the answers on **P. 207**

LESSON 6

It means...

-(ㄴ/는)다는 뜻이에요

Track 11

In Level 6 Lesson 2, we introduced how to say, "What do you mean?" or "What does that mean?" In this lesson, we will take a look at how to respond to these questions and form sentences to say "It means..." in Korean. The keyword you need to remember for this lesson is 뜻, the Korean word for "meaning".

뜻이에요. = It is (...) meaning.

Using "뜻이에요" alone is not enough. You need to include more information about what kind of meaning there is.

Verb stem + -(ㄴ/는)다는 + 뜻이에요. = It means...

Ex)
사람이 많다는 뜻이에요. = It means that there are a lot of people.
다 나았다는 뜻이에요. = It means that you have completely healed.

38

Conjugation

Noun + -(이)라는

Present tense:

Descriptive verb + -다는

Action verb + -ㄴ/는다는

Past tense:

Action/Descriptive verb + -았/었/였다는

Future tense:

Action/Descriptive verb + -(으)ㄹ 거라는

Track 11

뜻이에요 and 말이에요

Just like with the expressions for, "What do you mean?", 뜻 (= meaning) and 말 (= speech/language) are interchangeable with each other. 말이에요, however, has a stronger focus on the intended meaning of the speaker rather than the definition of the expression itself.

좋다는 뜻이에요. = It means that it is good.
좋다는 말이에요. = I am saying that it is good.

Sample Sentences

A: '완료'가 무슨 뜻이에요? = What does 완료 mean?
B: 끝났다는 뜻이에요. = It means that (something) has been finished.

A: '휴업*'이 무슨 뜻이에요? = What does 휴업 mean?

B: 일을 안 한다는 뜻이에요. = It means that you do not work.

    * 휴업 = to not provide service (When a restaurant is closed, you might see this on the door.)

    ** 휴가 = to not work / vacation

빨간불이 켜지면, 고장 났다는 뜻이에요.

= If the red light turns on, it means it is broken.

안 가고 싶다는 말이에요?

= Are you saying that you do not want to go?

그러면, 못 한다는 뜻이에요?

= Then, does it mean that they cannot do it?

Sample Dialogue

Track
12

경은: 석진 씨, 라이브 스트리밍이 무슨 뜻이에요?

Kyeong-eun: Seokjin, what does live streaming mean?

석진: 아, 인터넷으로 생방송을 한다는 뜻이에요.

Seokjin: It means to broadcast live through the Internet.

경은: 그런 건 누가 할 수 있어요?

Kyeong-eun: Who can do those kinds of things?

석진: 아무나 할 수 있어요.

Seokjin: Anyone can.

경은: 그러면 저도 할 수 있다는 뜻이에요?

Kyeong-eun: Then, do you mean I can do it, too?

Check the answers on **p. 207**

✏ Exercises for Lesson **6**

Translate the conversations below into Korean using the phrase(s) from the lesson.

1.

A: What does 완료 mean?

B: It means that (something) has been finished.

→

A: ....

B: ....

2.

A: Are you saying that you do not want to go?

B: Yes, I am saying that I do not want to go.

→

A: ....

B: ....

3.

A: All of a sudden, the red light turned on.

B: Really? If the red light turns on, it means it is broken.

→

A: ....

B: ....

4.

A: What does 휴업 mean?

B: It means that you do not work.

→

A: ....

B: ....

LESSON 7

Word Builder 15

점(點)

Word Builder lessons are designed to help you understand how to expand your vocabulary by learning and understanding some common and basic building blocks of Korean words. The words and letters introduced through Word Builder lessons are not necessarily all Chinese characters, or 한자. Though many of them are based on Chinese characters, the meanings can be different from modern-day Chinese. Your goal through these lessons is to understand how words are formed and then remember the keywords in Korean to expand your Korean vocabulary from there. You certainly do not have to memorize the Hanja characters, but if you want to, feel free!

Track 13

Today's key word element is 점.

The Chinese character for this is 點. There are many other Chinese characters (or Hanja) that are associated with 점, so keep in mind that not all of the words that have 점 in them are related.

The word 점 (點) is related to "point", "dot", or "spot".

Sample Expressions

강 (strong) + 점 (point) = 강점 强點 = strong point; strength

> **Ex)**
> 경화 씨, 경화 씨의 강점은 뭐예요?
> = Kyung-hwa, what is your strong point?

약 (weak) + 점 (point) = 약점 弱點 = weakness; weak point

장 (long, head) + 점 (point) = 장점 長點 = advantage; merit; virtue

Track 13

단 (short) + 점 (point) = 단점 短點 = drawback; shortcoming

초 (burn) + 점 (point) = 초점 焦點 = focus; focal point
* This is used a lot in photography.

> **Ex)**
> 초점이 맞아요.
> = It is in focus.
> 초점이 안 맞아요.
> = It is out of focus.

점 (point) + 수 (number) = 점수 點數 = score; mark; grade

Ex)

경화 씨, 학교 다닐 때 점수 좋았어요?

= Kyung-hwa, did you have good grades in school?

문 (ask) + 제 (topic) + 점 (point) = 문제점 問題點 = problem; drawback

관 (view) + 점 (point) = 관점 觀點 = point of view; viewpoint

요 (important) + 점 (point) = 요점 要點 = essential point; main point

Ex)

요점을 잘 찾아야 돼요.

= You need to find the main point.

Track 13

공 (one) + 통 (go through, to communicate, lead) + 점 (point) = 공통점 共通點 = something in common; common factors

차 (differ) + 이 (differ) + 점 (point) = 차이점 差異點 = difference

원 (origin) + 점 (point) = 원점 原點 = starting point; square one

Ex)

원점으로 돌아가다

= to go back to square one; to return to the starting point

학 (school, learn) + 점 (score) = 학점 學點 = school grade (usually university)

* 학점 is usually used for university-level while 점수 is used for grades below university.

Ex)

저는 학점이 안 좋았어요.

= My university grades were not good.

점 (point) + 자 (letter) = 점자 點字 = braille

득 (get) + 점 (point) = 득점 得點 = score; make a score (in a game)

점 (point) + 선 (line) = 점선 點線 = dotted line

Ex)

점선을 따라 오리세요.

= Cut along the dotted line.

점선을 따라 접으세요.

= Fold along the dotted line.

Sample Dialogue

Track 14

경화: 이번 과제는 두 소설의 공통점과
　　　차이점에 대해서 쓰는 거예요.

현우: 정말 어렵네요.

경화: 맞아요. 어떤 관점으로 보느냐에 따라
　　　다를 것 같아요.

현우: 학점을 잘 받기 위해서는 너무 길게
　　　쓰는 것보다 요점만 정리하는 게 좋을
　　　것 같아요.

Kyung-hwa: The assignment this time is to write about the similarities and differences of the two novels.

Hyunwoo: It sounds so difficult.

Kyung-hwa: Right. I think they can differ depending on the perspective.

Hyunwoo: If we want to get a high grade, I think it's better to summarize the main points rather than writing down everything.

✐ Exercises for Lesson **7**

Fill in the blanks with the appropriate Sino-Korean word from the lesson.

1. The key word element (   ) is related to "point", "dot", or "spot".

2. (   ) = advantage; merit; virtue

3. (   ) = focal point; focus

4. (   ) = starting point; square one

5. (   ) = essential point; main point

Check the answers on **p. 207**

LESSON **8**

I hope…, I wish…

-(으)면 좋겠어요

Track 15

In Level 6 Lesson 16, we introduced the various usages of the suffix -겠-. They include showing your assumptions about something, your intention to do something, as well as asking the other person whether they would like to do something. In the form -(으)면 좋겠어요, you will find two grammatical structures: one is -(으)면, and the other is -겠-. The usage of -겠- in -(으)면 좋겠어요 is for expressing your assumption or expectation about something.

-(으)면 = if
-겠- = that would be…, I would…, they would… (assuming)
좋다 + -겠- = 좋겠어요 = It would be nice; I would like it

So together, -(으)면 좋겠어요 takes the meaning of "It would be nice if…" or "I would like it if…" and can be also used when you want to say "I hope…" or "I wish…".

There are two different structures: one is Verb + -(으)면 좋겠어요 and the other is -(았/었/였)으면 좋겠어요. While one is in the present tense and the other is in the past tense, the meanings are very similar and identical in many cases. The past tense version, -(았/었/였)

49

으면 좋겠어요, is similar to using the past tense after "I wish", as in, "I wish it was snowing."

Ex)

빨리 끝나다 ＝ to finish quickly

빨리 끝나면 좋겠어요. ＝ I hope this finishes quickly.

＝ 빨리 끝났으면 좋겠어요. ＝ I hope this finishes quickly.

In English, there is a difference in meaning between "I hope" and "I wish", but that difference cannot be expressed through the structure -((았/었/였)으)면 좋겠어요. In order to express the nuance of "I wish... but I know it is not", you can use the structure -(았/었/였)으면 좋을 텐데... ("It would have been nice if...") or -아/어/여서 아쉽네요 ("Too bad it is...").

Track 15

What is 바라다?

When you look up the verb "to hope" in the dictionary, the first word is 바라다 or 희망하다. While they are correct "translations", it is more natural to use -(으)면 좋겠어요. If you want to use 바라다 or 희망하다, you can use the structure -기를 바라다 or -기를 희망하다, but the sentence will sound more like written language.

Sample Sentences

내일 사람들이 많이 왔으면 좋겠어요.

＝ I hope many people will come tomorrow.

＝ 내일 사람들이 많이 오면 좋겠어요.

비가 그쳤으면 좋겠어요.

＝ I hope it stops raining.

＝ 비가 그치면 좋겠어요.

제 선물, 마음에 들었으면 좋겠어요.

= I hope you like my present.

= 제 선물, 마음에 들면 좋겠어요.

주연 씨가 지각 안 했으면 좋겠어요.

= I would like it if Jooyeon would not be late for work.

= I hope Jooyeon is not late for work.

= 주연 씨가 지각 안 하면 좋겠어요.

제가 스무 살이었으면 좋겠어요.

= I wish I were 20 years old.

= 제가 스무 살이면 좋겠어요.

Track 15

내일도 날씨가 좋았으면 좋겠어요.

= I hope the weather is nice tomorrow as well.

= 내일도 날씨가 좋으면 좋겠어요.

Sample Dialogue

주연: 빨리 주말이 왔으면 좋겠어요.

예지: 맞아요. 오늘이 금요일이었으면
    좋겠는데 아직도 목요일이에요.

주연: 아... 일주일에 4일만 일했으면 좋겠다!

예지: 그래도 내일 하루만 더 출근하면
    주말이니까 우리 힘내요.

Jooyeon: I hope this weekend comes soon.

*Yeji: I know. I wish today was Friday, but it's still
    only Thursday.*

*Jooyeon: Ah… I wish we only needed to work four
    days a week.*

*Yeji: Let's keep it up as we only have to work
    tomorrow, and then it's going to be the
    weekend!*

✏ Exercises for Lesson *8*

Check the answers on **P. 208**

Translate each sentence into Korean and write it down on the lines provided.

1. I hope many people will come tomorrow.

....

2. I hope you like my present.

....

3. I wish I were 20 years old.

....

4. I hope the weather is nice tomorrow as well.

....

5. I hope Jooyeon is not late for work.

....

LESSON 9

Past Tense (Various Structures)

과거 시제 총정리

This lesson is a review and summary of the various types of past tense structures in the Korean language. There is only one basic past tense structure, the suffix -았/었/였-, but by combining it with other structures, you can create more sentences with specific meanings.

I. **-았/었/였-** *(Level 1 Lesson 17)*

Verb stem + -았/었/였- + -어요

> **Ex)**
> 사다 = to buy
> → 사 + -았어요 = 샀어요 = I (or someone else) bought it.
>
> 주다 = to give
> → 주 + -었어요 = 줬어요 = I gave it (to someone).

2. -았/었/였었어요

To further emphasize that one "had" done something in the past or before another action/state, some people add the suffix one more time, making it -았/었/였었어요 instead of -았/었/였어요.

Ex)

보다 = to see, to watch

→ 보 + -았어요 = 봤어요 = I saw.

→ 보 + -았- + -었어요 = 봤었어요 = I saw it a long time ago; I had seen it before.

3. -고는 했어요

To talk about something that you used to do regularly or habitually, you can use the ending -고는 했어요. When you use -고는 했어요 after a verb, it implies that you do not do it any longer.

Ex)

보다 = to watch

→ 보 + -고는 했어요 = 보고는 했어요 = I used to watch.

* You can even shorten this to "보곤 했어요."

밤 늦게까지 TV를 보고는 했어요.

= I used to watch TV until late at night.

* In spoken Korean, people will typically shorten it to, "보곤 했어요."

가끔 친구들을 만나고는 했어요.

= I used to meet my friends from time to time.

4. -(으)ㄴ *(Level 4 Lesson 26)*

-(으)ㄴ is the conjugation you can use after a verb stem to modify a noun. -(으)ㄴ needs to be followed by the noun that the verb modifies either as the object or the subject.

Ex)
마시다 = to drink
마시 + -ㄴ = 마신 = that I drank
어제 마신 커피 = the coffee that I drank yesterday

아까 이야기한 책
= the book I talked about earlier

Track
17

이 책을 쓴 사람
= the person who wrote the book

5. -던 *(Level 8 Lesson 4)*

-던 is also used after a verb to modify a noun. -(으)ㄴ is the basic verb ending for modifying nouns, but if you use -던, you can add the nuance of "used to" or "was doing but did not finish".

Ex)
마시다 = to drink
→ 마신 = (something) that I drank
→ 마시던 = (something) that I was drinking; (something) that I used to drink

그거 제가 마시던 커피예요.

= That is the coffee I was drinking (but did not finish).

어렸을 때 제가 좋아했던 만화책이에요.

= It is a comic book that I used to like when I was a kid.

6. -(으)ㄹ 뻔했어요 *(Level 5 Lesson 1)*

When you say -(으)ㄹ 뻔했어요 after a verb stem, it means that something "almost happened" or that you "almost did" something.

Track
17

> **Ex)**
> 잊다 = to forget
>   → 잊 + -을 뻔했어요 = 잊을 뻔했어요. = I almost forgot.
>
> 넘어지다 = to fall down (on the ground)
>   → 넘어지 + -ㄹ 뻔했어요 = 넘어질 뻔했어요. = I almost fell down.

너무 놀라서 소리를 지를 뻔했어요.

= I was so surprised that I almost screamed.

너무 무거워서 떨어뜨릴 뻔했어요.

= It was so heavy that I almost dropped it.

7. -아/어/여 봤어요 *(Level 4 Lesson 12)*

-아/어/여 보다 means "to try doing something" or "to give something a try". By using this in

57

the past tense, you can say "I have tried doing + something + before" or "I have done + something + before" in Korean.

Ex)

듣다 = to listen

→ 듣 + -어 보다 → 들어 보다 (irregular conjugation)

→ 이 노래 들어 봤어요? = Have you heard this song (before)?

이거 읽어 봤어요? = Have you read this? / Have you tried reading this?

8. -(으)ㄴ 적 있어요

Track 17

-(으)ㄴ 적 있어요 is used after verb stems to mean "I have done + something + before", to talk about one's experience. You can also use -아/어/여 본 적 있다 to mean the same thing, using the -아/어/여 보다 structure.

Ex)

배우다 = to learn

→ 배우 + ㄴ 적 있어요 = 배운 적 있어요. = I have learned it before. / I have the experience of learning it.

중국어 배운 적 있어요? = Have you learned Chinese before?

중국어 배워 본 적 있어요? = Have you tried learning Chinese before?

여기 와 본 적 없어요. = I have not been here before.

= 여기 온 적 없어요.

= 여기 안 와 봤어요.

Sample Dialogue

호영: 우와! 민재 씨, 그림을 정말 잘 그리시네요! 그림 배운 적 있어요?

민재: 네, 어릴 때 배웠었어요. 주말마다 아빠랑 같이 그림을 그리곤 했어요.

호영: 그렇구나! 그림이 너무 예뻐서 한참 봤어요.

민재: 감사해요. 오랜만에 어릴 때 생각이 나서 그려 봤어요.

Hoyoung: Wow! Minjae, you are so good at drawing! Have you learned how to draw before?

Minjae: Yes, I have when I was little. I used to paint with my dad on weekends.

Hoyoung: I see! I was looking at your drawing for a while, it's so beautiful.

Minjae: Thanks. I was reminded of my childhood for the first time in a while, so I just tried to paint some.

Tense Structures, and Situational Expressions

✏ Exercises for Lesson **9**

Translate the phrases and sentences below into Korean.

1. the book I talked about earlier

....

2. I bought it.

....

3. Have you tried learning Chinese before?

....

4. Have you read this?

....

5. It was so heavy that I almost dropped it.

....

6. I used to meet my friends from time to time.

....

Check the answers on **p. 208**

Improve Proficiency with Idiomatic Phrases,

LESSON **10**

Advanced Idiomatic Expressions 2

귀 (Ear)

This is an Advanced Idiomatic Expressions lesson related to 귀, the ear! In order to fully understand and use the expressions introduced in this series, it is essential that you understand the grammatical structure of the sentences. When you come across a grammar point with which you are unfamiliar, please go back and review the related lessons.

Track 19

Keyword: 귀 = ear

I. 귀가 밝다 = to have good ears

The literal translation of 밝다 is "to be bright", but the actual meaning of 귀가 밝다 is that you have good ears. "To hear well" or "can hear well" is 잘 들을 수 있다 or 잘 들리다 in Korean, but it is more natural to say that your 귀 is 밝다 in many cases. It refers to your hearing capabilities, not whether you can hear a particular sound in a certain situation. In the case of the latter, you can say, "잘 안 들려요" to mean, "I cannot hear it clearly (due to other noise or sound)."

61

Ex)

젊었을 때는 저도 귀가 밝았는데, 지금은 작은 소리는 잘 안 들려요.

= I used to have good ears when I was young, too, but I cannot hear quiet sounds now.

2. 귀를 기울이다 = to pay attention to a sound or to what someone says

▷ 기울이다 = to tilt; to make something lean

When you want to pay attention to a certain sound, you naturally want to move your ears closer to the source of the sound. Even though you lean your whole body, in Korean you say that you lean your ear toward something. 귀를 기울이다 can mean both "trying to hear something well" and "paying attention to what someone says".

Track 19

Ex)

귀를 기울여서 잘 들어 보세요.

= Pay close attention to what you hear.

아이들이 선생님이 해 주는 이야기를 귀를 기울여서 듣고 있었어요.

= The children were listening to the story their teacher was telling them with full attention.

3. 귀에 대고 속삭이다 = to whisper into someone's ears

▷ 대다 = to put something close to something else

▷ 속삭이다 = to whisper

You could just say 귀에 속삭이다 to say "to whisper into someone's ears", but the part 대고 is used to describe the action of going closer to someone before whispering. 귀에 대다 means to put something close to or touch the ear, and in this case, it is someone's mouth.

Ex)

귀에 대고 속삭이지 말고 크게 말해요.

= Do not whisper to each other secretly. Speak loudly (to everybody).

* You can say this if two people are whispering to each other and you want them to speak up, or if someone is whispering to you and they do not need to whisper.

4. **귀먹다** = to be deaf, to be unable to hear

When someone cannot hear something well, you can use the expression 귀먹다 or 귀가 먹다. The word 먹다 is usually to eat, but not in this case. 귀가 먹다 can be used for someone who cannot hear due to old age, but you can also hear people say, "귀먹었어(요)?" to someone who cannot seem to understand or care about what they hear, even though they physically are able to hear.

Track 19

Ex)

저 귀 안 먹었어요. 조용히 말해요.

= I am not deaf. Speak quietly.

너 귀먹었어? 왜 이렇게 못 알아들어?

= Did you go deaf? Why don't you understand what I am saying?

5. **귀가 간지럽다** = to feel like someone is talking behind one's back

 ▷ 간지럽다 = to feel itchy

There is no way to spy on everybody and know when people talk about you, but you can use the expression 귀가 간지럽다 when you refer to the fact that people talk about you when you are not around. It is usually used in the past tense, after you find out that people talked about you in your absence.

Ex)

어쩐지 오늘 귀가 간지러웠어요.

= No wonder my ears were itchy today.

= I see that you talked about me.

6. 귀가 얇다 = to be easily influenced by what others say

▷ 얇다 = to be thin

If your ears are thin, it will be easy for words to penetrate your brain. 귀가 얇다 is a figurative way of saying that someone is easily influenced by what he or she hears.

Track 19

Ex)

그 사람은 귀가 얇아서 설득하기 쉬워요.

= He is easily influenced by what people say, so he is easy to persuade.

7. 귀에 못이 박히도록 (듣다) = to have heard something too much already

▷ 박히다 = to be embedded; to be stuck

▷ -도록 = to the extent of...

못 usually means "cannot" or "nail", but in this case, it refers to a callus, or the hardened skin on your hand due to heavy use. When you hear something over and over again, your ear will (figuratively) harden, so when you say 귀에 못이 박히도록 (듣다), it means that you have (heard) something over and over again, so much that it makes you sick or upset.

Ex)

그 얘기는 귀에 못이 박히도록 들었어요.

= I have heard that story so much. I do not need to hear it again.

내가 귀에 못이 박히도록 말했는데* 왜 안 듣니?

= I have told you so many times, but why are you not listening?

* People also often say **귀에 못이 박히도록 말하다/이야기하다** to mean "to tell (someone) a million times".

Sample Dialogue

Track
20

예지: 민종 씨가 어제 또 에어컨 안 끄고
　　　퇴근했더라고요.

캐시: 또요? 예지 씨가 그렇게 귀에 못이
　　　박히도록 얘기했는데도요?

예지: 네. 제 말에 귀를 기울이지 않는 것 같아요.

캐시: 근데 좀 조용히 이야기해야 될 것 같아요.
　　　민종 씨가 귀가 엄청 밝거든요.

Yeji: Min-jong left the office without turning the
　　　AC off again yesterday.

Cassie: Again? You've told him about that a
　　　million times!

Yeji: I know. I don't think he pays attention to
　　　what I say.

Cassie: I think we need to lower our voice a
　　　little bit, by the way. Min-jong has really
　　　good ears.

✏️ Exercises for Lesson *10*

Fill in the blanks with the appropriate idioms with 귀 from the lesson.

1. (   )

   = to feel like someone is talking behind one's back

2. (   )

   = to be deaf; to be unable to hear

3. (   )

   = to pay attention to a sound or to what someone says

4. (   )

   = to have heard something too much already

5. (   )

   = to be easily influenced by what others say

6. (   )

   = to have good ears

Check the answers on **p. 208**

BLOG

Ulleungdo
(울릉도)

If you were to do a quick search to see how many islands are located off the coast of South Korea, you would find a fairly decent number; there are 3,215 islands! However, most of these are uninhabited and some of them we are not even able to visit. While we might not be able to visit all of them, there are some amazing islands we can visit. Most people have probably heard of Jeju Island, especially if you have been studying with Talk To Me in Korean as we have talked about the different folktales around Jeju as well as some of their amazing food. But today, I am going to talk about a different spot that many people may not have even thought to visit.

Ulleungdo is located in the East Sea off the coast of Korea and is in Gyeongsangbuk Province. Since my time in Korea, I have only been here once. Actually, many of my Korean friends have never even visited Ulleungdo. The reason is that due to weather conditions surrounding the island, it can be quite difficult to visit, which is something we will come back to later on in this blog. So, how do we get there?

I went with a group of friends and we had to take a bus from Seoul to Gangneung. From there, we took a ferry to Ulleungdo. When trying to book a ferry, make sure to do a bit of research as some boats can be a bit more expensive. One of the cheapest ones was around 48,000 won and that was just to get to the island. You also have to purchase a ticket to get back to the mainland which was a bit more expensive. You will also want to keep an eye on the weather. We got a little worried as we received a few texts prior to our arrival at the port that the trip could be canceled due to the rough wind and waves. Luckily, our trip was not canceled and we were on our way. The ride is a few hours long and if you are prone to getting seasick, I recommend buying some motion sickness medicine or drink to help. I bought some just in case and did not have any problems.

When we arrived, we decided to check out some cliffs nearby and boy was it impressive! We got to walk along the cliffs on this pathway that was carved into the rocks. At one point, there was a bridge that takes you over this gap between some of the cliffs and allows you to see into a cave with the water crashing against the rocks below you. It was such a surreal moment and one I will never forget.

Afterwards, we went and checked out Turtle Rock. This is a rock on the island that is massive in size and looks similar to the shape of a turtle. Since we had been on a boat just about all morning and it was lunchtime, we then headed to get some food. Ulleungdo is known for its fresh seafood so we went to try some of their raw fish. The plate we were given was massive and the food was delicious. However, for most people who visit Ulleungdo, there is one goal everyone hopes to achieve. That is visiting Dokdo.

We were told prior to our trip that there was a good chance we would not actually get to visit Dokdo. It is one of the hardest islands to visit in Korea. One family told us they were just about to reach the shore of Dokdo when the captain of the boat came over the intercom and said that due to the ocean currents, they would not be able to dock and must turn around. As you can probably tell, we were a bit nervous but we were still in high spirits. The weather just needed to stay calm till the morning and we would be good to go. Well, as luck would turn out, we got a text in the morning letting us know that the weather conditions were not good and we must cancel our trip to Dokdo. A bit disappointed, we headed to Manghyang Peak. If you are in Ulleungdo, I highly recommend checking out this peak and taking the cable car up

to the top. The view is absolutely stunning and it was a great way to lift our spirits. Once we reached the top, we did a bit of hiking to reach the peak where on a clear day, you can actually see Dokdo. My friends and I stood there for a bit soaking in the view. This is one trip I will never forget, and who knows, maybe one day I can go back and actually step on Dokdo with my own feet.

If you are planning on checking out Ulleungdo, here are a few other places you may want to check out. We were on a bit of a time squeeze so we could not see everything, but I have been told these are also some beautiful spots to visit.

Dodong Lighthouse (도동등대)
Yaksu Park (약수공원)
Dokdo Observation Platform (독도전망대)
Seonginbong (성인봉)
Bongnae Falls (봉래폭포)

Written by Johnny Bland

LESSON **11**

Sentence Building Drill 12

Sentence Building Drill 12

Track 21

In this series, we focus on how you can use the grammatical rules and expressions that you have learned so far to train yourself to comfortably and flexibly make more Korean sentences.

We will start off with THREE key sentences, then practice changing parts of these sentences so that you do not end up just memorizing the same three sentences. We want you to be able to be as flexible as possible with the Korean sentences that you can make.

Key Sentence (1)

내일 친구들이랑 만날 것 같은데, 날씨가 좋았으면 좋겠어요.

= I think I will meet my friends tomorrow, so I hope the weather will be nice.

Key Sentence (2)

어제 운동을 많이 한 데다가, 일도 늦게 끝나서, 눕기가 무섭게 잠들었어요.

= On top of working out a lot, work also finished late yesterday, so I fell asleep as soon as I lay down.

Improve Proficiency with Idiomatic Phrases,

Key Sentence (3)

제가 어제 읽던 책인데, 어차피 다 못 읽을 것 같아요.

＝ It is a book that I was reading yesterday, but I do not think I will be able to finish reading it anyway.

Expansion & Variation Practice with Key Sentence (1)

0. Original Sentence:

내일 친구들이랑 만날 것 같은데, 날씨가 좋았으면 좋겠어요.

＝ I think I will meet my friends tomorrow, so I hope the weather will be nice.

1.

내일 친구들이랑 만날 것 같은데 ＝ I think I will meet my friends tomorrow, so/but...

아마 내일도 비가 올 것 같은데 ＝ I think it will probably rain again tomorrow, so/but...

별로 안 어려울 것 같은데 ＝ I do not think it will be too difficult, so/but...

아마 안 될 것 같은데 ＝ I think it probably will not work, so/but...

물어봐야 알 것 같은데 ＝ I think I will have to ask them, so/but...

Track
21

2.

날씨가 좋았으면 좋겠어요. ＝ I hope the weather will be nice.

비가 안 왔으면 좋겠어요. ＝ I hope it will not rain.

사람들이 별로 없었으면 좋겠어요. ＝ I hope there are not too many people.

빨리 시작했으면 좋겠어요. ＝ I hope it will start soon.

그 사람들은 안 왔으면 좋겠어요. ＝ Those people, I hope they do not come here.

Expansion & Variation Practice with Key Sentence (2)

0. Original Sentence:

어제 운동을 많이 한 데다가, 일도 늦게 끝나서, 눕기가 무섭게 잠들었어요.

= On top of working out a lot, work also finished late yesterday, so I fell asleep as soon as I lay down.

I.

운동을 많이 한 데다가, 일도 늦게 끝나서

= On top of working out a lot, work finished late too, so...

일이 바쁜 데다가, 감기에도 걸려서

= On top of work being busy, I also got a cold, so...

날씨도 좋은 데다가, 휴일이어서

= On top of the weather being nice, it is a holiday, so...

Track 21

저는 원래 잠이 많은 데다가, 요즘에 항상 일찍 일어나서

= I usually need a lot of sleep; on top of that, I always get up early these days, so...

2.

눕기가 무섭게 잠들었어요.

= I fell asleep as soon as I lay down.

문을 열기가 무섭게 사람들이 들어왔어요.

= People came in as soon as we opened the door.

비디오를 올리기가 무섭게 코멘트가 달리기 시작했어요.

= Comments started being posted as soon as we uploaded the video.

집에 오기가 무섭게 다시 나갔어요.

= He went out again as soon as he came home.

Expansion & Variation Practice with Key Sentence (3)

0. Original Sentence:

제가 어제 읽던 책인데, 어차피 다 못 읽을 것 같아요.

= It is a book that I was reading yesterday, but I do not think I will be able to finish reading it anyway.

1.

제가 어제 읽던 책인데 = It is a book that I was reading yesterday, so/but...

예전에 자주 가던 곳인데 = It is a place I used to go to often before, so/but...

제가 입던 옷인데 = These are the clothes I used to wear, so/but...

제가 일하던 곳인데 = It is a place I used to work at, so/but...

2.

Track
21

어차피 다 못 읽을 것 같아요.

= I do not think I will be able to finish reading it anyway.

어차피 사람들 다 못 앉을 것 같아요.

= I do not think everybody will be able to sit down anyway.

어차피 시간 안에 못 끝낼 것 같아요.

= I do not think you will be able to finish in time anyway.

어차피 좀 기다려야 될 것 같아요.

= I think you will have to wait a little anyway.

Sample Dialogue

경은: 내일 일찍 퇴근해야 해서, 일을 빨리
　　　끝낼 수 있었으면 좋겠어요.

현우: 일이 많아요? 그럼 경은 씨 업무를
　　　저한테 좀 주세요. 저는 내일 할 일도
　　　없는 데다가, 늦은 시간에 약속이
　　　있어서 어차피 사무실에 늦게까지 있을
　　　것 같아요.

경은: 정말요? 그럼 이거 제가 하던 업무인데,
　　　내일 마무리해 줄 수 있어요?

현우: 와, 말 꺼내기가 무섭게 부탁하시네요!
　　　네, 제 메일로 보내 주세요.

Kyeong-eun: I have to go home early tomorrow. I hope I will be able to get my work done quickly.

Hyunwoo: Do you have a lot of work? Then, give me some of your work. I don't have much to do tomorrow and I think I am going to stay late in the office anyway as I have plans late at night.

Kyeong-eun: Really? In that case, could you finish up this task I have been working on tomorrow?

Hyunwoo: Oh, wow. You made a request as soon as I finished my sentence! Yes, please send it to my email.

✏ Exercises for Lesson 11

Translate each phrase or sentence into Korean and then write it on the lines provided below.

1. On top of working out a lot, work also finished late yesterday, so...

....

2. I think I will have to ask them, so/but...

....

3. I think you will have to wait a little anyway.

....

4. It is a book that I was reading yesterday, but I do not think I will be able to finish reading it anyway.

....

5. On top of work being busy, I also got a cold, so I fell asleep as soon as I lay down.

....

Check the answers on **p. 208**

LESSON 12

Present Tense (Various Structures)

현재 시제 총정리

Track 23

This lesson is a review and summary of the various types of present tense structures in the Korean language.

1. -아/어/여 *(Level 1 Lesson 16)*

Verb stem + -아/어/여 + -요

Ex)

사다 = to buy

→ 사 + -아요 = 사요. = I buy it. / She buys it. / They buy it. / Buy it.

주다 = to give

→ 주 + -어요 = 줘요. = I give it (to someone). / They give it (to someone). / Give it to me.

78

저는 매일 운동해요.

= I exercise every day.

저는 한국어를 혼자서 공부해요.

= I study Korean by myself.

2. -시- + -어요 *(Level 5 Lesson 2)*

The suffix -시- is used to make the sentence honorific when you are talking to or about someone for whom you want to show respect.

Verb stem + -시- + -어요

* When you combine -시- and -어요, it is supposed to become -셔요, but that was only used in the old days, so people nowadays say -세요 instead of -셔요.

Track 23

Ex)

가다 = to go

→ 가 + -시- + -어요 = 가셔요 = 가세요 = He goes. / She goes. / Please go.

모르다 = to not know

→ 모르 + -시- + -어요 = 모르셔요 = 모르세요 = He does not know. / She does not know.

3. -고 있다 *(Level 2 Lesson 10)*

-고 있다 is used after verb stems to form present progressive sentences. 있다 is then conjugated to match the context or the intended tense of the sentence.

Ex)

공부하다 = to study

→ 공부하 + -고 있다

→ 공부하고 있어요. = I am studying. / They are studying.

지금 뭐 하고 있어요?

= What are you doing now?

서점에 가고 있어요.

= I am going to a bookstore.

Track 23

4. -고 싶다 (Level 1 Lesson 13)

-고 싶다 is used to express "I want to...".

Ex)

보다 = to see

→ 보 + 고 싶다

→ 보고 싶어요. = I want to see. / I miss you.

뭐 하고 싶어요?

= What do you want to do?

밖에 나가고 싶어요.

= I want to go outside.

5. -(으)ㄹ 수 있다 *(Level 2 Lesson 17)*

-(으)ㄹ 수 있다 is used to express "can" or "be able to".

Ex)

찾다 = to look for; to find

→ 찾 + -(으)ㄹ 수 있다

→ 찾을 수 있어요. = I can look for it. / I can find it.

여기 주차할 수 있어요?

= Can I park here?

여기 주차할 수 있어요.

= You can park here.

Track 23

이거 읽을 수 있어요?

= Are you able to read this?

이거 읽을 수 있어요.

= I can read this.

6. -아/어/여야 되다 *(Level 2 Lesson 20)*

You can use the -아/어/여야 되다 ending to express "have to", "should", or "must".

Ex)

가다 = to go

→ 가 + -아야 되다 = 가야 되다

→ 가야 돼요. = I have to go.

이거 먼저 해야 돼요.

= I need to do this first.

조심해야 돼요.

= You have to be careful.

7. -지 않다, 안 *(Level 1 Lesson 21)*

Track 23

You can form negative sentences by adding -지 않다 after the verb stem or 안 before the verb.

Ex)

이상하다 = to be strange

→ 이상하 + -지 않다

→ 이상하지 않아요 = It is not strange.

→ 안 + 이상하다

→ 안 이상해요. = It is not strange.

* In spoken Korean, 안 is more common. In written and formal language, -지 않아요 is equally common.

이거 안 비싸요.

= This is not expensive.

그거 별로 안 좋아요.

= It is not that good.

8. -지 마세요 *(Level 2 Lesson 30)*

-지 마세요 is used after verb stems to tell someone not to do something.

Ex)

먹다 = to eat

→ 먹 + -지 마세요 = 먹지 마세요. = Do not eat it.

걱정하지 마세요.

= Do not worry.

늦지 마세요.

= Do not be late.

Track 23

9. -아/어/여요 *(Level 3 Lesson 16)*

-아/어/여요 looks the same as the plain present tense, but it can be used to form "Let us" sentences as well.

Ex)

하다 = to do

→ 하 + -여요 = 해요. = Let us do it.

같이 해요.

= Let us do it together.

지금 가요.

= Let us go now.

83

10. -(으)ㄴ 것 같다 *(Level 4 Lesson 27)*

같다 originally means "to be the same" or "to seem like", but when expressing your opinion about something, you can use -(으)ㄴ 것 같다 to say "I think...".

Ex)
좋다 = to be good
→ 좋 + -은 것 같다
→ 좋은 것 같아요. = I think it is good.

이상한 것 같아요.
= I think it is strange.

Track
23

그 사람 착한 것 같아요.
= I think he is a nice person.

그 사람들 착한 것 같아요.
= I think they are nice people.

저 착한 것 같아요.
= I think I am a nice person.

11. -(으)ㄹ 수도 있다 *(Level 3 Lesson 22)*

When you want to say that something "might" or "could" happen, you can use the structure -(으)ㄹ 수도 있다.

Ex)

늦다 = to be late

→ 늦 + -(으)ㄹ 수도 있다

→ 늦을 수도 있어요. = I might be late. / They might be late.

석진 씨가 알 수도 있어요.

= Seokjin might know.

오늘 집에 있을 수도 있어요.

= I might stay at home today.

Track 23

Sample Dialogue

Track
24

캐시: 에밀리 씨, 무슨 공부 해요?

에밀리: 한국어 공부하고 있어요.

캐시: 한국어 어렵지 않아요? 저도 한국어
　　　배우고 싶어요.

에밀리: 별로 안 어려워요. 저랑 같이 공부해요.

캐시: 그럴까요? 에밀리 씨가 저 좀 가르쳐
　　　주세요.

에밀리: 좋아요. 근데 저도 많이 잘하진 않아요.
　　　더 공부해야 돼요.

Cassie: Emily, what are you studying?

Emily: I am studying Korean.

Cassie: Isn't it hard? I also want to learn
　　　Korean.

Emily: It's not that difficult. Let's study together.

Cassie: That sounds good. Please teach me
　　　Korean.

Emily: Sure. But I am not that good at it. I have
　　　to study more.

✏ *Exercises for Lesson 12*

Make a sentence that ends in -요 by combining the phrases, and then translate them into English.

1. 보다 + -고 싶다 →

2. 읽다 + - (으)ㄹ 수 있다 →

3. 가다 + -아/어/여야 되다 →

4. 좋다 + -은 것 같다 →

5. 늦다 + -(으)ㄹ 수도 있다 →

Translate each phrase or sentence into Korean and write it on the lines provided.

6. It is not strange.

....

7. Let us go now.

....

8. I think I am a nice person.

....

Check the answers on **P. 208**

Tense Structures, and Situational Expressions

LESSON 13

Word Builder 16

주(主)

Word Builder lessons are designed to help you understand how to expand your vocabulary by learning and understanding some common and basic building blocks of Korean words. The words and letters introduced through Word Builder lessons are not necessarily all Chinese characters, or 한자. Though many of them are based on Chinese characters, the meanings can be different from modern-day Chinese. Your goal through these lessons is to understand how words are formed and then remember the keywords in Korean to expand your Korean vocabulary from there. You certainly do not have to memorize the Hanja characters, but if you want to, feel free!

Today's key word element is 주.

The Chinese character for this is 主. There are many other Chinese characters (or Hanja) that are associated with 주, so keep in mind that not all of the words that have 주 in them are related.

The word 주 (主) is related to "king", "owner", "main", or "autonomous".

주 (owner) + 인 (person) = 주인 主人 = owner

Ex)

이거 주인 누구예요?

= Who does this belong to?

주 (main) + 인 (person) + 공 (fair) = 주인공 主人公 = main character

주 (main) + 요 (important) = 주요 主要 = major; important

* 주요 is a noun, but it is often used before another noun as a modifier, such as 주요 도시 (major cities), 주요 장면 (important scenes), etc. If you add -하다 to 주요, it becomes a descriptive verb (infinitive form of an adjective), 주요하다. If you want to use it as a modifier, you should conjugate it into 주요한.

Track
25

주 (main) + 류 (flow) = 주류 主流 = mainstream

주 (main) + 력 (force, power) = 주력 主力 = main force

주 (main) + 동 (movement) + 자 (person) = 주동자 主動者 = prime mover; leader (of a protest)

* This word is not often used these days. It is usually used when talking about demonstrations or movements, or to refer to a student who leads others to bully another student.

주 (main) + 원 (source) + 인 (cause) = 주원인 主原因 = leading cause; main reason

주 (main) + 원 (source) + 료 (count) = 주원료 主原料 = main material

* This is usually for chemical products.

주 (owner) + 부 (wife) = 주부 主婦 = housewife; homemaker

주 (owner) + 장 (give) = 주장 主張 = opinion; insistence

주 (owner) + 도 (lead) + 권 (power, authority) = 주도권 主導權 = leadership; initiative
* Sometimes people use this word when a couple is about to get married to see who will decide on things in the household.

주 (owner) + 권 (power) = 주권 主權 = sovereignty

주 (main) + 특 (special) + 기 (skill) = 주특기 主特技 = specialty; special ability

주 (main) + 목 (eye) + 적 (target) = 주목적 主目的 = primary goal; main purpose
* Usually used in formal situations.

Ex)
여기 온 주목적이 뭡니까?
= What is your main purpose in coming here?

주 (owner) + 관 (view) = 주관 主觀 = one's own opinion

Related Vocabulary
고집 固執 = stubbornness

주 (owner) + 어 (language) = 주어 主語 = subject (grammar)

Sample Dialogue

경화: 이 브랜드의 주력 상품이 이 장미 향수래요.

경은: 와, 향이 참 좋네요. 장미 향수니까 주원료는 당연히 장미꽃이겠죠?

경화: 네, 맞아요. 요즘 인기 있는 드라마에 주인공이 이 향수 쓰는 장면 나왔잖아요.

경은: 아! 그래서 이 향수 인기가 이렇게 많아졌군요.

Kyung-hwa: They say the signature product of this brand is this rose perfume.

Kyeong-eun: It has a beautiful scent. Since it's a rose perfume, its main ingredient must be roses, right?

Kyung-hwa: Yes, that's right. There was a scene in a popular TV drama with the main actress using this perfume.

Kyeong-eun: Oh, so that's why the perfume has also gained a lot of popularity.

✏ Exercises for Lesson 13

Fill in the blanks with the appropriate Sino-Korean word from the lesson.

1. The key word element (   ) is related to "king", "owner", "main", or "autonomous".

2. (   ) = main character

3. (   ) = housewife; homemaker

4. (   ) = opinion; insistence

5. (   ) = subject (grammar)

6. (   ) = leadership; initiative

Check the answers on **p. 208**

LESSON **14**

Advanced Situational Expressions 2

찬성할 때
(Agreeing in Korean)

Welcome to another lesson in the series Advanced Situational Expressions. In this lesson, we will introduce how to agree with someone. In addition to the basic, "Yes (= 네)", there are a lot of expressions you can use to make your Korean sound more natural and fluent. Be sure to practice all of the phrases introduced in this lesson, and try using them at least once, as soon as you can.

Track
27

1.
네. = Yes.

2.
맞아요. = That is right. / That is correct.
(formal) 맞습니다.

3.
그렇죠. = That is right. / That is true.
(formal) 그렇습니다.

Track 27

4.

좋아요. = Good. / Sounds good. / I like the idea.

(formal) 좋습니다.

5.

물론이죠. = Of course. / Sure. / For sure.

(formal) 물론입니다.

* 물론 literally means, "No discussion".

6.

당연하죠! = Of course!

7.

그럼요! = Sure!

* This is actually a rhetorical question because it literally means, "If not, then what?"

** The standard pronunciation of 그럼요 is [그러묘], but most people pronounce it as [그럼뇨].

8.

바로 그거죠! = Exactly! / That is what I am saying!

(formal) 바로 그겁니다!

9.

좋은 생각이에요. = That is a good idea.

(formal) 좋은 생각입니다.

10.

저도 그렇게 생각해요. = I think so too. / My thoughts exactly.

(formal) 저도 같은 생각입니다.

11.

그렇게 하면 되겠네요. = That will do. / That will work.

12.

알겠어요. = I got it. / I see.

* 알았어요 has a similar meaning but is not as polite.

13.

그럼 그렇게 해요. = Then let us do it that way.

(formal) 그럼 그렇게 하시죠.

14.

안 될 거 없죠. = Why not? / There is no reason we cannot do it that way.

* "왜 안 돼요?" has a similar meaning; both of these come from English expressions.

Track 27

15.

찬성이에요. = I agree.

(formal) 찬성입니다.

* You can also add 저는 and say, "저는 찬성이에요" or, "저는 찬성해요" especially when you would like to imply that you somewhat agree but you are not sure what others think.

Sample Dialogue

저 지금 가요~

주연: 석진 씨, 점심 먹을 거예요?	*Jooyeon: Seokjin, are you going to have lunch?*
석진: 당연하죠. 지금 나갈까요?	*Seokjin: Of course, do you want to go out now?*
주연: 경화 씨가 지금 사무실로 오고 있대요. 경화 씨 오면 같이 나가요.	*Jooyeon: Kyung-hwa says she is on her way to the office. Let's go with her when she gets here.*
석진: 알겠어요.	*Seokjin: Fair enough.*
주연: 앗! 지금 밖에 비 와요! 그냥 시켜 먹는 건 어때요?	*Jooyeon: Jeez, it's raining outside! What about just ordering delivery food?*
석진: 좋아요. 안 될 거 없죠.	*Seokjin: Sure, why not?*

✏ *Exercises for Lesson 14*

Agree with the following suggestions using the Korean expressions from the lesson. Write down all of the phrases that are suitable for each situation.

1. Would you like a cup of coffee?

....

2. Can I borrow your pen?

....

3. Do you agree with my opinion?

....

4. Is this your address?

....

5. Can we stop by a convenience store?

....

6. Can we get the one that is red?

....

LESSON **15**

Future Tense (Various Structures)

미래 시제 총정리

This lesson is a review and summary of the various types of future tense structures in the Korean language. There are mainly two basic future tense structures, -(으)ㄹ 거예요 and -(으)ㄹ게요, but by combining them with other structures, you can create more sentences with specific meanings.

I. -(으)ㄹ 거예요 *(Level 2 Lesson 1)*

Verb stem + -(으)ㄹ 거예요

> **Ex)**
> 사다 = to buy
> → 사 + -(으)ㄹ 거예요 = 살 거예요. = I (or someone else) will buy it.
>
> 주다 = to give
> → 주 + -(으)ㄹ 거예요 = 줄 거예요. = I (or someone else) will give (something to someone).

2. -(으)ㄹ게요 *(Level 3 Lesson 6)*

Verb stem + -(으)ㄹ게요

* You cannot use this when talking about other people.

Ex)

보다 = to see

→ 보 + -(으)ㄹ게요 = 볼게요. = I will check.

기다리다 = to wait

→ 기다리 + -(으)ㄹ게요 = 기다릴게요. = I will wait.

3. -(으)ㄹ 계획이에요

Track 29

계획 means "plan" or "scheme", so if you say "Verb stem + -(으)ㄹ 계획이에요", it means you plan to do something or you are planning to do something.

Ex)

번역하다 = to translate

→ 번역하 + -(으)ㄹ 계획이에요 = 번역할 계획이에요. = I am planning to translate.

옮기다 = to move to a different spot

→ 옮기 + -(으)ㄹ 계획이에요 = 옮길 계획이에요. = I am planning to move (something to a different spot).

* You can use this when talking about moving to another city or when moving a box from one spot to another.

4. -(으)ㄹ 예정이에요

예정 means "schedule" or "being scheduled", so it is similar to 계획, but 예정 is used in more formal situations. 계획 is also a little more certain.

Ex)

시작되다 = to begin; to be started

→ 시작되 + -(으)ㄹ 예정이에요 = 시작될 예정이에요. = It is scheduled to begin. / It is going to start.

이 공연은 10분 후에 시작될 예정이에요. = This performance is scheduled to begin in 10 minutes.

방문하다 = to visit (formal)

→ 방문하 + -(으)ㄹ 예정이에요 = 방문할 예정이에요. = I am scheduled to visit. / It is in his schedule to visit.

Track 29

5. -(으)ㄹ 것 같아요 *(Level 4 Lesson 27)*

When you say "Verb stem + -(으)ㄹ 것 같아요", it means you think that something will happen or you will do something, but you are not completely sure. -(으)ㄹ 것 같아요 is usually the Korean translation of the English expression "I think". People often say 거 instead of 것 when they speak quickly.

Ex)

곧 도착하다 = to arrive soon

→ 곧 도착하 + -(으)ㄹ 것 같아요 = 곧 도착할 것 같아요. = I think we will arrive soon.

잘되다 = to go well

→ 잘되 + -(으)ㄹ 것 같다 = 잘될 것 같아요. = I think it will go well.

6. -(으)ㄹ지도 몰라요 and -(으)ㄹ 수도 있어요 *(Level 3 Lesson 22)*

When you say "Verb stem + -(으)ㄹ지도 몰라요" or "Verb stem + -(으)ㄹ 수도 있어요", it means that you MIGHT do something or something MIGHT happen. The two expressions are very similar and almost always interchangeable.

Ex)

안 가다 = to not go

→ 안 가 + -(으)ㄹ지도 몰라요 = 안 갈지도 몰라요. = I might not go.

→ 안 가 + -(으)ㄹ 수도 있어요 = 안 갈 수도 있어요. = I might not go.

Track
29

7. -(으)ㄹ까 생각 중이에요

In this structure, the -(으)ㄹ까 part is like a question for oneself. "Verb stem + -(으)ㄹ까" is followed by 생각 중이에요, which means, "I am thinking" or "I am in the middle of a thought."

Ex)

일본어를 배우다 = to learn Japanese

→ 일본어를 배우 + -(으)ㄹ까 생각 중이에요 = 일본어를 배울까 생각 중이에요. = I am thinking of learning Japanese.

101

8. -(으)ㄹ까 해요

-(으)ㄹ까 해요 has the same meaning as -(으)ㄹ까 생각 중이에요. Since the -(으)ㄹ까 part itself is usually sufficient to express that the person is asking oneself, the following part does not always have to be 생각 중이에요. It can be 고민 중이에요, 생각하고 있어요, or other phrases, but the most commonly used short form is 해요.

> **Ex)**
> 일본어를 배울까 생각 중이에요. → 일본어를 배울까 해요. = I am thinking of learning Japanese. / I want to learn Japanese.
>
> 집에 갈까 생각 중이에요. → 집에 갈까 해요. = I am thinking of going home.
> * Remember, you cannot say, "집에 가는 것을 생각 중이에요" because you are not thinking of the process of traveling back home.

Track 29

9. -(으)려고 해요 *(Level 5 Lesson 8)*

-(으)려고 해요 is used after verb stems to express one's intention to do something or when something seems about to occur.

> **Ex)**
> 포스터가 떨어지다 = the poster falls off
> → 포스터가 떨어지 + -(으)려고 해요 = 포스터가 떨어지려고 해요. = The poster is about to fall off.
> * You can also say, "포스터가 떨어질 것 같아요."

Sample Dialogue

Track
30

석진: 현우 씨, 저희 10분 뒤에 영화관으로
　　 출발할 예정이에요.

현우: 사무실에서 영화관까지 오는 데
　　 얼마나 걸릴 것 같아요?

석진: 아마 30분 정도 걸릴 거예요. 그런데
　　 더 늦어질지도 몰라요.

현우: 알겠어요. 그럼 영화관 앞에 있는
　　 카페에서 기다리고 있을게요.

Seokjin: Hyunwoo, we are going to head to the
　　 movie theater in 10 minutes.

Hyunwoo: How long do you think it will take you
　　 from the office to the movie theater?

Seokjin: It may take around 30 minutes. But it
　　 might take longer than that.

Hyunwoo: Okay. Then, I will be waiting in the cafe
　　 in front of the movie theater.

✏ Exercises for Lesson 15

Make a sentence by combining the phrases and translate them into English.

1. 번역하다 + -(으)ㄹ 계획이에요   →

2. 안 가다 + -(으)ㄹ지도 몰라요   →

3. 일본어를 배우다 + -(으)ㄹ까 생각 중이에요   →

4. 포스터가 떨어지다 + -(으)려고 해요   →

Translate each phrase or sentence into Korean ending in -요, and then write it on the lines provided.

5. I will wait.

....

6. I think we will arrive soon.

....

7. I am thinking of going home.

....

8. I might not go.

....

LESSON **16**

Advanced Idiomatic Expressions 3

가슴 (Chest, Heart, Breast, Mind)

This is an Advanced Idiomatic Expressions lesson related to 가슴, the chest, heart, breast, or mind. In order to fully understand and use the expressions introduced in this series, it is essential that you understand the grammatical structure of the sentences. When you come across a grammar point with which you are unfamiliar, please go back and review the related lessons.

Keyword: **가슴** = chest, heart, breast, mind

I. **가슴이 아프다** = one's heart aches; it makes one sad

This could mean that you have some pain in your chest, but normally if you say this, people will understand it as you are sad or that something is breaking your heart. You can also say **마음이 아프다**.

Ex)

저는 이런 기사를 읽으면 너무 가슴이 아파요.

= I am so sad when I read articles like this.

= If I read articles like this, I am so sad.

2. 가슴이 두근거리다 = to be thrilled; one's heart is pounding

두근거리다 can also be used alone to mean "to be thrilled" or "one's heart is pounding", but it is often used together with 가슴이. When you have something very exciting or absolutely nerve-wracking coming up soon, such as confessing something to someone or going on stage for a performance, you can use this expression.

Track 31

Ex)

어젯밤에 가슴이 두근거려서 잠을 많이 못 잤어요.

= I could not sleep a lot last night because I was so excited.

* 두근두근 = pit-a-pat (onomatopoeia for a beating heart)

3. 가슴이 뛰다 = one's heart beats; one's heart races; to be happily excited and motivated

When you are excited about something and your heart is beating faster than normal, you can say 가슴이 뛰다. It can be used for both good and bad situations, but is more commonly used for good situations, such as when your heart is racing because you saw someone you like, or when you are about to achieve something that you have wanted for a long time.

Ex)

지금 가슴이 너무 뛰어서 말이 안 나와요.

= Right now I am so excited that I cannot speak.

4. **가슴이 답답하다** = to feel a pressure on one's chest; to feel heavy with worry

  ▷ **답답하다** = to be stuffy; to be stifling

답답하다 can be used to refer to a stuffy environment, but it can also be used to talk about a situation or something that does not work as well as one wants. 가슴이 답답하다 is mixture of both of these meanings. When there is something that is not working out like you wish, you can feel that your 가슴이 답답하다.

Ex)
요즘에 걱정이 많아서 가슴이 답답해요.
= I have a lot of things to worry about these days, so I feel a pressure on my chest.

5. **가슴이 내려앉다** = to be greatly surprised; to be startled; one's heart sinks

Track 31

내려앉다 means to sink or to collapse, so when your heart or chest suddenly "sinks" due to surprise, sadness, or disappointment, you can use the expression 가슴이 내려앉다. This is usually used in a bad situation. People also use 가슴이 철렁하다 to say the same thing. 철렁 here is an onomatopoeia used to describe the sound of one's heart sinking.

Ex)
그 소식 듣고 정말 가슴이 내려앉았어요.
= My heart sank when I heard that news.

6. **부푼 가슴을 안고** = with a pounding heart

  ▷ **안다** = to hug

부풀다 means "to inflate", so 부푼 가슴 is an inflated chest or inflated heart. This means your heart or mind is full of hope and excitement, so the expression 부푼 가슴을 안고 refers to the attitude in which you are dealing with things with great excitement and high hopes. This expression, however, tends to be used more often in written language. Remember this as a fixed phrase.

Ex)

부푼 가슴을 안고 10년 전에 서울로 이사 왔어요.

= I moved to Seoul 10 years ago, full of excitement for what I would be doing.

7. 가슴에 와닿다 = something touches one's heart; to hit home

Track
31

When something comes along and touches your heart, it means it hits "close to home" and you are moved. In that case, you can use the expression 가슴에 와닿다. On the contrary, however, if a story or a movie does not "hit home" and you are not touched by it, you can say 가슴에 와닿지 않다. Since 닿다 means "to reach" or "to touch", if you say 가슴에 닿다, you are saying something physically touches your chest.

Ex)

왜인지 모르겠지만 이 이야기는 가슴에 와닿지 않아요.

= I do not know why, but this story does not touch my heart.

8. 가슴에 맺힌 한을 풀다 = to resolve one's deep sorrow

한 is deep resentment or deep sorrow. 맺히다, which means "to form", is usually used with 눈물 (tears), 이슬 (dew), 땀 (sweat), or 한 (resentment). 풀다 means to resolve, so 가슴에

맺힌 한을 풀다 means to resolve some long overdue deep sorrow, usually by finally doing something that one has not been able to do or by being forgiven by someone.

Ex)

저희 어머니는 드디어 가슴에 맺힌 한을 풀었어요.

= My mother finally got/achieved what she had been hoping for.

9. 가슴 벅차다 = to be overwhelmed (with joy); one's heart is overflowing with joy

When you are overwhelmed with joy and your heart is "full", you can say 가슴이 벅차다.

Track 31

Ex)

제 친구가 올림픽에서 금메달을 따서 정말 가슴이 벅차요.

= My heart is overflowing with joy because my friend won a gold medal in the Olympic Games.

10. 가슴 깊이 후회하다 = to deeply regret

In fact, you can omit the word 가슴 and just say 깊이 후회하다 to mean the same thing, but by adding the word 가슴, you give the expression a stronger nuance.

Ex)

그때 제가 했던 말을 가슴 깊이 후회하고 있어요.

= I am deeply regretting what I said back then.

11. 가슴 깊이 뉘우치다 = to deeply repent

This expression is very similar to 가슴 깊이 후회하다, except 뉘우치다 is closer to repenting and realizing one's fault.

Ex)
가슴 깊이 뉘우치고 있어요. 용서해 주세요.
= I am deeply repenting what I did. Please forgive me.

12. 가슴이 콩닥콩닥 (뛰다) = one's heart is pounding

Track 31

콩닥콩닥 is an onomatopoeia that describes the sound of a pounding heart but also a mimetic word that describes how the heart pounds in a small and cute way. Other words that describe the same kind of movement or sound in a bigger scale or in a more serious way are 쿵쾅쿵쾅 or 쿵덕쿵덕.

Ex)
좋아하는 가수를 봐서 가슴이 콩닥콩닥 뛰었어요.
= I saw my favorite singer so my heart was pounding.

Sample Dialogue

잭: 유나 씨, '말리와 나'라는 영화 봤어요?

유나: 네, 봤어요. 마지막에 너무 가슴이
아파서 정말 많이 울었어요.

잭: 저도요. 저는 지금 강아지를 키우고
있으니까 더 가슴에 와닿았어요.

유나: 아, 진짜 그랬겠어요.

Jack: Yuna, did you see the movie called 'Marley
& Me'?

Yuna: Yes, I did. The last scene was so sad. It
made me cry a lot.

Jack: Me, too. It really touched my heart since I
also have puppies.

Yuna: Oh, it must have.

111

✏ *Exercises for Lesson 16*

Fill in the blanks with the appropriate idioms with **가슴** *from the lesson.*

1. (   ) = to be thrilled; one's heart is pounding

2. (   ) = to feel a pressure on one's chest; to feel heavy with worry

3. (   ) = to deeply regret

4. (   ) = to resolve one's deep sorrow

5. (   ) = to deeply repent

6. (   ) = to be greatly surprised; to be startled; one's heart sinks

Check the answers on **p. 209**

LESSON **17**

If only it is not…

-만 아니면

In this lesson, we will take a look at the structure -만 아니면, which means "if only it's not…" or "if only you were not…". This is used in situations where you talk about something that you would be willing to do, but you cannot because of some reason. For example, you can use -만 아니면 in sentences like, "If you were not my brother, I would not hang out with you" or, "I would totally meet you for coffee, but I have work to do."

Track
33

Structure

(1) Noun + -만 아니면 + Verb stem + -(으)ㄹ 텐데요
= If only it were not + Noun, I would + Verb
= If only it were not for + Noun, I would + Verb
= If only I did not have + Noun, I would + Verb

This is used when you want to say that you would do something only if A were not B.

113

Ex)

오늘이 월요일만 아니면 거기 갈 텐데요.

= If only today were not Monday, I would go there.

* This is basically saying, "I cannot go there because it is Monday today." However, by using "-만 아니면", you are expressing you are really sorry.

숙제만 아니면 지금 갈 텐데요.

= If only I did not have my homework, I would go.

(2) Noun + -만 아니면 + Verb stem + -았/었/였을 거예요

= If only it were not + Noun, I would have + Past participle

= If only it were not for + Noun, I would have + Past participle

= If only I did not have + Noun, I would have + Past participle

Track
33

Ex)

친구만 아니면 경찰에 신고했을 거예요.

= If only she were not my friend, I would have reported her to the police.

오늘이 친구 생일만 아니면 그냥 집에 있었을 거예요.

= If only today were not my friend's birthday, I would have just stayed home.

* In this situation, you did not really want to go out, but since it was your friend's birthday, you felt you had to.

(3) Noun + -만 아니면...

= If only it were not + Noun...

= If only it were not for + Noun...

= If only I did not have + Noun...

When what you would have done is obvious and can be easily guessed by the listener, you can just omit the rest of the sentence.

Ex)

직장 상사만 아니면...

= If only he were not my boss at work...

Sample Sentences

그 사람이 제 친구 친척만 아니면...

= If only he were not related to my friend...

이것만 아니면...

= If only this did not exist...

Track
33

공사 소리만 아니면 잘 잤을 거예요.

= If only it were not for the construction noise, I would have slept well.

여기가 친구 집만 아니면, 지금 잠들었을 거예요.

= If only I were not at a friend's house, I would have fallen asleep.

저희 담임 선생님만 아니면, 따졌을 거예요.

= If only he were not my homeroom teacher, I would have started an argument.

Sample Dialogue

Track
34

진영: 현우 씨가 전화를 안 받아요.

경화: 그래요? 운동하고 있는 것만 아니면 받을 텐데요.

진영: 운동하고 있나 봐요.

경화: 그런가 보네요. 체육관만 아니면 받았을 거예요.

Jinyoung: Hyunwoo is not answering the phone.

Kyung-hwa: He's not? He would have picked up the phone if he was not working out.

Jinyoung: I think he is working out.

Kyung-hwa: I guess so. If he weren't in the gym, he would have answered the phone.

✏ Exercises for Lesson 17

Translate each phrase or sentence into Korean using -만 아니면 *and write it on the lines provided.*

1. If only this did not exist...

....

2. If only he were not my boss at work...

....

3. If only he were not related to my friend...

....

4. If only it were not for the construction noise, I would have slept well.

....

5. If only today were not my friend's birthday, I would have just stayed at home.

....

Check the answers on **p.209**

Tense Structures, and Situational Expressions

LESSON **18**

In the same way that…, Just like someone did…

-(으/느)ㄴ 대로

Track 35

In today's lesson, we will look at the grammatical structure -(으/느)ㄴ 대로. This is used when you want to describe how something is done in the same way as another action, or how it remains in the same state as the current. You can say things like, "Leave it as is", "Did you do as I told you?", or, "I wrote down what I heard" using this structure.

Conjugation

Past tense: Verb stem + -(으)ㄴ 대로

Present tense: Verb stem + -(느)ㄴ 대로

Ex)

보다 = to see

→ 본 대로 = the way you saw it; just the way you saw it; as you saw it

→ 보는 대로 = the way you see it; just the way you see it; as you see it

하다 = to do

→ 제가 한 대로 = the way I did it; just like I did it; as I did it

→ 제가 하는 대로 = the way I do it; just like I do it; as I do it

Let us take a look at some commonly used phrases containing -(으/느)ㄴ 대로

1. 아는 대로 = just the way one knows

Ex)

아는 대로 말해 주세요.

= Please tell me everything you know.

= Please tell me how you know of it (without changing anything).

Track 35

아는 대로 쓰세요.

= Just write whatever you know.

= You do not have to add or change anything, just write what you know.

2. 말한 대로 = just the way one said

Ex)

제가 말한 대로 했어요?

= Did you do it the way I told you?

= Did you do as I said?

예지 씨가 말한 대로 했는데, 안 됐어요.

= We did as Yeji said, but it did not work.

= We did it just as Yeji told us to, but it did not go well.

3. 들은 대로 = just like one heard

Ex)

들은 대로 이야기해 주세요.

= Tell me what you heard.

= Tell me exactly as you heard it.

들은 대로 잘 전달했어요.

= I delivered the message well.

= I passed on what I heard accurately.

Other Usages and Forms of -(으/느)ㄴ 대로 or -대로

Track
35

I. -(느)ㄴ 대로 meaning "as soon as"

→ You can use -(느)ㄴ 대로 after a verb stem to mean "as soon as".

Ex)

도착하다 = to arrive

→ 도착하는 대로 전화해 주세요. = Call me as soon as you arrive.

* You can use what we learned in previous lessons as well, such as, "도착하자마자 전화

해 주세요." or, "도착하면 바로 전화해 주세요."

2. Verb stem + -던 대로

→ You can use -던 대로 instead of -(으)ㄴ 대로 to talk about a past action or state that was

not finished or was repeated.

Ex)

하다 = to do, 평소 = usual times, 평소에 = usually

→ 평소에 하던 대로 하세요. = Just do as you usually do. / Just do it in the way you have always done it.

* You can also say 평소에 하는 대로, but by using 하던 대로, you are showing it was a habit.

3. 이대로, 그대로, and 저대로

→ Combined with 이, 그, and 저, you can say "just like this" or "just like that" with 이대로, 그대로, and 저대로. The meanings are affected by the original meanings of the words 이, 그, and 저.

이대로 = just the way it is now; keeping the current state

저대로 = just like that is over there now; keeping the current state of that thing/person over there

그대로 = just the way it is (In this case, whatever you are referring to is closer to the listener, far away from you.)

Track
35

4. Noun + -대로

→ When you add -대로 after a noun, it means "following + Noun" or "just like how [something] goes". Please note that there should be no space between the noun and -대로.

Ex)

제 말대로 = like I said; following what I said

▷ 제 = my (polite)

▷ 말 = words, saying, what one says

예언대로 = just as the prophecy said; just like the prediction said

▷ 예언 = prophecy, prediction

121

Sample Dialogue

Track 36

예지: 이번에 광고 포스터가 주문한 대로 안 나왔어요. 이대로는 못 쓸 것 같아요.

소희: 어? 제가 말한 대로 전달했는데 이렇게 나왔어요?

예지: 네. 저희가 생각한 대로 안 나왔네요. 다시 주문할까요?

소희: 네. 이번에는 전화로 주문하지 말고 평소에 하던 대로 이메일로 주문해 주세요.

Yeji: The ad posters did not come out as we had ordered this time. I don't think we can use them.

Sohee: What? Even though you told them just the way I told you, it came out this way?

Yeji: Yes, they didn't come out the way we thought. Do you want me to order them again?

Sohee: Yes. But, this time, please order the posters via email as we always do, not by phone.

✏ *Exercises for Lesson 18*

Fill in the blanks using -(으/느)ㄴ/던 대로.

1. (   ) 쓰세요.

    = Just write whatever you know.

2. (   ) 전화해 주세요.

    = Call me as soon as you arrive.

3. 예지 씨가 (   ) 했는데, 안 됐어요.

    = We did as Yeji said, but it did not work.

4. 평소에 (   ) 하세요.

    = Just do as you usually do.

5. (   ) 잘 전달했어요.

    = I passed on what I heard accurately.

Check the answers on **p.209**

LESSON **19**

Even if I would have to…, Even if that means I have to…

-는 한이 있더라도

Track 37

Today's grammar point, -는 한이 있더라도, is used when you want to say "even if that means I have to…" or "even if I end up… -ing…", meaning that you would take risks or try your best to achieve a desired result.

> ### Conjugation
>
> Verb stem + -는 한이 있더라도
>
> = even if I end up + Verb-ing
>
> = even if that means I have to + Verb

By adding -는 after a verb stem, you are turning it into an adjective. The word 한 means "case" or "situation", so the literal translation of this structure is "even if there is a situation where ABC happens, (I will do XYZ)". The phrase that follows is usually about something that one is determined to do, cannot do, or has to do. When -는 한이 있더라도 is used in a sentence, that sentence usually ends with -수 없어요 (cannot do), -아/어/여야 돼요 (have to), or -(으)ㄹ 거예요 (will).

Ex)

나중에 후회하는 한이 있더라도

= Even if that means we will regret it later

다치는 한이 있더라도

= Even if I might end up getting injured

지는 한이 있더라도

= Even if we might end up losing

Sample Sentences

무대에서 쓰러지는 한이 있더라도 공연을 취소할 수는 없어요.

= Even if it means I might collapse on the stage, we cannot cancel the performance.

Track
37

여행 계획을 다 취소하는 한이 있더라도 지금 수술을 받아야 돼요.

= Even if that means we have to cancel all the travel plans, you need to get this surgery now.

회사를 그만두는 한이 있더라도 할 말은 해야겠어요.

= Even if I end up quitting the job because of this, I have to say what I have to say.

약속에 많이 늦는 한이 있더라도 화장은 꼭 하고 가야 돼요.

= Even if I might end up being very late for the meeting, I must put my makeup on before I go.

금방 고장 나서 버리는 한이 있더라도 일단 사야겠어요.

= Even though this might end up breaking and I will have to throw it away, I have to buy it now (and think about it later).

125

Sample Dialogue

예지: 퇴근 안 해요?

석진: 부장님이 밤새는 한이 있더라도 이거 다 끝내고 집에 가라고 하셨어요.

예지: 진짜요? 아직 많이 남았어요?

석진: 조금밖에 안 남았어요. 제가 저녁을 굶는 한이 있더라도 오늘 안에 꼭 다 끝내고 집에 갈 거예요.

Yeji: You're not getting off work?

Seokjin: The general manager asked me to make sure to finish this before going home, even if that means I have to stay up all night.

Yeji: Seriously? Is there still a lot left?

Seokjin: No, just a little bit. I will definitely get this done tonight and go home, even if I have to skip dinner.

✏ Exercises for Lesson 19

Check the answers on **p.209**

Fill in the blanks using -는 한이 있더라도.

1. Even if that means we will regret it later

= ( )

2. Even if I might end up getting injured

= ( )

3. Even if we might end up losing

= ( )

4. Even if I end up quitting the job because of this, I have to say what I have to say.

= 회사를 ( ), 할 말은 해야겠어요.

5. Even if it means I might collapse on the stage, we cannot cancel the performance.

= 무대에서 ( ), 공연을 취소할 수는 없어요.

6. Even if that means we have to cancel all the travel plans, you need to get this surgery now.

= 여행 계획을 다 ( ), 지금 수술을 받아야 돼요.

127

LESSON **20**

Sentence Building Drill 13

Sentence Building Drill 13

Track 39

In this series, we focus on how you can use the grammatical rules and expressions that you have learned so far to train yourself to comfortably and flexibly make more Korean sentences.

We will start off with THREE key sentences, then practice changing parts of these sentences so that you do not end up just memorizing the same three sentences. We want you to be able to be as flexible as possible with the Korean sentences that you can make.

Key Sentence (1)

아무리 바빠도, 원칙대로 해야 돼요.

= No matter how busy you are, you have to do it by the rules.

Key Sentence (2)

나중에 바꾸는 한이 있더라도, 지금은 이렇게 했으면 좋겠어요.

= Even if we might end up changing it later, I hope we just go with this for now.

Key Sentence (3)

회사 일만 아니면 저도 호주로 여행을 갔을 거예요.

= If only I did not have this work from my job, I would have gone to Australia to travel, too.

Expansion & Variation Practice with Key Sentence (1)

0. Original Sentence:

아무리 바빠도, 원칙대로 해야 돼요.

= No matter how busy you are, you have to do it by the rules.

1.

아무리 바빠도 = No matter how busy you are...

아무리 힘들어도 = No matter how tired you are...; No matter how difficult it is...

Track 39

아무리 친구가 중요해도 = No matter how important friends are to you...

아무리 재미없는 이야기여도 = No matter how boring the story is...

* You can also say, "아무리 이야기가 재미없어도".

아무리 비싸도 = No matter how expensive it is...

2.

원칙대로 해야 돼요. = You have to do it by the rules.

마음대로 하세요. = Do as you please.

제가 말한 대로 하세요. = Do as I said.

들은 대로 이야기해 주세요. = Tell me exactly what you heard.

약속대로 해 주세요. = Please do it as you promised you would.

Expansion & Variation Practice with Key Sentence (2)

0. Original Sentence:

나중에 바꾸는 한이 있더라도, 지금은 이렇게 했으면 좋겠어요.

= Even if we might end up changing it later, I hope we just go with this for now.

1.

나중에 바꾸는 한이 있더라도 = Even if we have to change it later...

조금 늦는 한이 있더라도 = Even if this makes me a little late for it...

내일 다시 오는 한이 있더라도 = Even if that means I might end up coming back again tomorrow...

집에 못 가는 한이 있더라도 = Even if it means I might not be able to go home...

다른 사람들이 욕하는 한이 있더라도 = Even if it means other people might criticize me...

2.

지금은 이렇게 했으면 좋겠어요. = This time, I hope we do it like this.

사람들이 많이 왔으면 좋겠어요. = I wish a lot of people would come.

날씨가 좋았으면 좋겠어요. = I hope the weather will be nice.

창문을 닫았으면 좋겠어요. = I hope they close the window.

조용한 데로 갔으면 좋겠어요. = I hope we go somewhere quiet.

Expansion & Variation Practice with Key Sentence (3)

0. Original Sentence:

회사 일만 아니면 저도 호주로 여행을 갔을 거예요.

= If only I did not have this work from my job, I would have gone to Australia to travel, too.

1.

회사 일만 아니면 = If only it had not been for the work from my job...

회의만 아니면 = If only it had not been for the meeting...

가족 행사만 아니면 = If only I did not have to go to this family event...

컴퓨터 바이러스만 아니면 = If only it had not been for the computer virus...

주차 요금만 아니면 = If only it had not been for the parking fees...

2.

저도 호주로 여행을 갔을 거예요. = I would have gone to Australia to travel, too.

저도 그렇게 말했을 거예요. = I would have said that, too.

예지 씨도 이걸 골랐을 거예요. = Yeji would have chosen this, too.

제프 씨도 좋다고 했을 거예요. = Jeff would have said good.

안 된다고 했을 거예요. = I would have said no.

잘됐을 거예요. = It would have gone well.

Track 39

Sample Dialogue

Track
40

캐시: 석진 씨, 잠 많이 못 잤어요?
아까부터 계속 졸고 있는 거
봤어요.

석진: 네. 어제 밤새 미드 봤거든요.

캐시: 아무리 재밌어도 밤새 보느라고 잠
못 자면 피곤하잖아요.

석진: 아, 저는 일단 보기 시작하면 한
시간 자고 출근하는 한이 있더라도
끝까지 봐야 돼요. 사실 출근만
아니면 시즌 2, 3 계속 봤을 거예요.

*Cassie: Seokjin, didn't you get enough sleep last
night? I saw you kept dozing off.*

Seokjin: No, I watched an American drama all night.

*Cassie: No matter how entertaining it is, if you don't
get enough sleep because you watched it all
night, you are bound to be tired.*

*Seokjin: For me, once I start watching a drama,
I have to finish it, even if that means I
can only sleep one hour before going to
work. Actually, I would have kept watching
seasons 2 and 3 if it had not been for work.*

✏ Exercises for Lesson **20**

Translate each phrase or sentence into Korean and write it on the lines provided.

1. Do as you please.

....

2. No matter how busy you are...

....

3. No matter how expensive it is...

....

4. I wish a lot of people would come.

....

5. Even if it means I might not be able to go home...

....

Check the answers on **p. 209**

BULGOGI RECIPE
(불고기)

If you are like most people who visit Korea, there is one item that you may have heard a lot about and probably cannot wait to try for yourself. That dish is bulgogi (불고기, 불 = fire, 고기 = meat).

As the name suggests, bulgogi refers to a Korean meat dish cooked over fire. Before the 1800s, Korean people used to skewer meat and cook it directly over a fire, but around 1800, people started to cook meat on a griddle or a grill. At that time, they would cut the meat into chunkier pieces when cooking and call it neobiani (너비아니). There is not much definitive research on when exactly the word "bulgogi" began being used instead of "neobiani", but people assume that it was right before or after the restoration of Korean independence.

The term 불고기 first entered the 1947 edition of the Dictionary of Korean Language as "meat grilled directly over a charcoal fire". It was later included in the American English lexicon in 1961.

However, what we call bulgogi nowadays is slightly different from what used to be called neobiani. It is made from thin slices of sirloin or other prime cuts of beef. Before cooking the meat, it is first marinated in a mixture of soy sauce, sugar, sesame oil, garlic, and ground pepper. Depending on the person, this mixture could also include scallions, ginger, onions, or mushrooms. To cook it, traditionally, it is grilled over a fire, but recently many places have started to pan-cook this delicious meat. Most places will also offer sides like lettuce to wrap up the meat and ssamjang to add before shoving it into your mouth.

This is a dish you can find all over Korea with each province adding their own flavor. Some might even change the meat from beef to pork. There are also different ways to serve bulgogi; you might get it over rice, which is called 불고기덮밥 in Korean. If I am being honest, this is my favorite way to eat it. I just love mixing the meat with the rice as it seems to balance out the meal. Some places will serve bulgogi as a soup of sorts, called 뚝배기불고기, which is great for the cold winter days here in Korea. As you can see, there are many different ways to prepare the meat as well as many different ways to serve it. So, let's jump into what you really want to know.

How can I make this at home?

Bulgogi Recipe

- Ingredients

Bulgogi Sauce

½ of an Onion

½ of an Apple

100ml Soy Sauce

100ml Water

3 Tablespoons Sugar (White or Brown)

1 Tablespoon of Minced Garlic

1 Pinch of Ground Pepper

1 Stalk of Green Onion

Bulgogi

200g Bulgogi (Thinly-sliced Beef)

½ of an Onion

½ of a Carrot

1 Stalk of Green Onion

- How to Prepare Bulgogi

In order to make your very own bulgogi, you first need to prepare the sauce. You will need to cut the onion, apple, and green onion into small pieces and place them in a blender. Then, add the soy sauce, water, sugar, minced garlic, and ground pepper. Blend it all up until it is smooth.

Now, let's move onto the meat and vegetables you will be cooking along with the sauce. Cut the carrot into strips, cut the onions lengthwise, and cut the green onion into thin strips.

Turn on your stove if you are going to cook the bulgogi on a pan. Once the pan is hot, it is time to add the vegetables. Make sure to cook them well before adding the beef. Once the vegetables are cooked, add the beef and sauce and mix everything together. Once the meat is cooked well, you can add it to a plate and dig in. Oh, and if you wanted to add a bit of decoration, use some of the strips of green onion to place on top of your bulgogi.

If you are planning on having a few people over, this is a great surprise dish. Add a bit of rice on the side and I am sure it will be a hit with your guests!

Written by Johnny Bland

우와!

벌써 Lesson 20까지 공부했네요!

다음 레슨에는 어떤 재미있는 표현이 기다리고 있을까요?

.

LESSON **21**

Advanced Idiomatic Expressions 4

머리 (Head, Hair)

This is an Advanced Idiomatic Expressions lesson related to 머리, the head or hair. In order to fully understand and use the expressions introduced in this series, it is essential that you understand the grammatical structure of the sentences. When you come across a grammar point with which you are unfamiliar, please go back and review the related lessons.

Keyword: **머리** = head, hair

I. 머리가 좋다/나쁘다 = to be smart/stupid

The literal translation is that your "head" is good or bad, but the figurative translation is that someone is "smart" or "not smart". Instead of 머리가 나쁘다, you can also say 머리가 안 좋다. They mean the same thing.

Ex)

그 사람은 머리는 좋은데 노력을 안 해요.

= He is smart, but he does not make any effort.

2. 머리를 쓰다 = to use one's brain; to think (as opposed to just act); to do brain work

머리를 쓰다 is often used when thinking things through as opposed to just acting spontaneously without thinking too much. This phrase can also mean "to have the intelligence to do things in a smart or efficient way".

Ex)

힘으로만 하지 말고 머리를 좀 써 보세요.

= Do not try to do it just by strength, but think a little bit (about how to solve this problem).

Track 41

3. 머리를 굴리다

= to put one's brain to work; to use one's head to try to find a solution to a problem

머리를 굴리다 literally means "to roll one's head", but when used in context, it means "to try to come up with a solution to a problem by putting one's brain to work". This is a rather casual expression, so it can be considered rude to use it about or to someone older than you.

Ex)

아무리 머리를 굴려 봐도 답이 안 나와요.

= No matter how hard I try (to think of a solution), I cannot find an answer (or solution).

141

4. **잔머리(를) 굴리다** = to think of excuses; to get oneself out of a situation

잔머리(를) 굴리다 is similar to 머리를 굴리다, but by adding the word 잔 (adjective form of 잘다, meaning "little" or "small") to 머리, you add the nuance of "excuses" or "trying to find shortcuts/lazy ways to get out of a situation". Just like 머리를 굴리다, this is not appropriate to use with someone for whom you need to show respect or be formal.

Ex)
잔머리 굴리지 말고 열심히 일해.

= Stop trying to find ways to work less. Just work hard.

= Do not think of an excuse to not work. Get your work done.

Track 41

5. **머리가 깨질 것 같다** = to have a very bad headache; to have a splitting headache
   ▷ 깨지다 = to break

It does not mean that your head is really going to break or split, it just means that you have a really bad headache. You can also say, "머리가 깨질 것처럼 아파요", the literal meaning of which is, "My head hurts as if it is going to be broken."

Ex)
요즘 잠을 많이 못 잤더니 머리가 깨질 것처럼 아파요.

= I have not been sleeping enough lately, so I have a splitting headache.

6. **머리가 (잘) 안 돌아가다** = cannot think well; cannot think straight; one's brain is slow
   ▷ 돌아가다 = to go around; to go back; to spin

142

When you say that your brain or head "spins" in Korean, like a motor or a hard drive in a computer, it means that your brain "works" or that you are thinking. So when you say that your brain "does not spin very well", you mean that you cannot think clearly, straight, or well for the moment.

Ex)

피곤해서 머리가 안 돌아가요. 바람 좀 쐬고 올게요.

= I am tired so I cannot think straight. I will go get some fresh air.

7. 머리가 복잡하다 = cannot think straight; to have a lot of concerns in one's head

▷ 복잡하다 = to be complicated; to be complex

Track 41

When someone says that his or her "head" is "complicated" in Korean, you can assume that it means a lot of thoughts and concerns are cluttering the person's brain. 머리가 복잡하다 usually has a negative connotation, so be careful when you use it!

Ex)

요즘에 걱정되는 일이 많아서 머리가 복잡해요.

= I am worried about a lot of things these days, so my head is full of concerns.

8. 머리를 스치다 = an idea (or thought) that flashes through one's mind

스치다 is originally "to graze" or "to brush past". When you walk past someone and your shoulder touches the other person's shoulder very lightly, you use the verb 스치다. Therefore, when an idea (아이디어) or a thought (생각) occurs to you, you can say 머리를 스치다.

143

Ex)

재미있는 생각이 머리를 스쳤어요.

= I just thought of an interesting idea.

= An interesting idea just flashed through my head.

9. 머리가 멍하다 = one's mind is blank; to be disoriented

If you find yourself in a situation where your mind goes completely blank due to any number of reasons - whether it be stress, confusion, or fatigue - you can say 머리가 멍하다 in Korean to express your situation.

Track 41

Ex)

여기 너무 시끄러워서 머리가 멍해요.

= It is so noisy here that I cannot think.

10. 머리가 띵하다 = to feel dizzy; one's brain feels numb

You can use 머리다 띵하다 for when you feel dizzy as well as when you have a headache that makes your brain feel numb.

Ex)

갑자기 일어섰더니 머리가 띵해요.

= I stood up suddenly, and now I feel dizzy.

11. **머리가 크다** = to start thinking like a grown-up and making mature judgements

You can say **머리가 크다** about a person whose head is physically big, but you can also use the word **크다** to mean "to grow up". In this case, **머리가 크다** means "to start thinking like a grown-up" or "to feel like someone has grown up and does not want to listen to what older people tell him/her".

Ex)

이제 애들이 머리가 커서 말을 안 들어요.

= The children have grown, so now they do not listen to what I say.

Track 41

145

Sample Dialogue

유정: 나 잠깐 바람 좀 쐬고 올게. 머리가
　　　잘 안 돌아가네.

예서: 또? 너 일하기 싫어서 그러지?
　　　잔머리 굴리지 마.

유정: 아니야! 어제 잠을 많이 못 자서
　　　진짜 머리가 깨질 것 같아.

예서: 알겠어. 그럼 좀 쉬다가 와.

*Yujeong: Let me go get some air. It feels like my brain
has stopped working.*

*Ye-seo: Again? You just don't want to work, huh? Stop
trying to find ways to work less.*

*Yujeong: No! I have a splitting headache because I
didn't get enough sleep last night.*

Ye-seo: Okay then. Get some rest.

✎ Exercises for Lesson 21

Check the answers on **p. 210**

Fill in the blanks with the appropriate idioms with 머리 *from the lesson.*

1. (   )

    = to start thinking like a grown-up and making mature judgements

2. (   )

    = to think of excuses (to get oneself out of a situation)

3. (   )

    = to use one's brain; to think (as opposed to just act); to do brain work

4. (   )

    = to be smart

5. (   )

    = an idea (or thought) that flashes through one's mind

Tense Structures, and Situational Expressions

LESSON **22**

Word Builder 17

상 (上)

Track 43

Word Builder lessons are designed to help you understand how to expand your vocabulary by learning and understanding some common and basic building blocks of Korean words. The words and letters introduced through Word Builder lessons are not necessarily all Chinese characters, or 한자. Though many of them are based on Chinese characters, the meanings can be different from modern-day Chinese. Your goal through these lessons is to understand how words are formed and then remember the keywords in Korean to expand your Korean vocabulary from there. You certainly do not have to memorize the Hanja characters, but if you want to, feel free!

Today's key word element is 상.

The Chinese character for this is 上. There are many other Chinese characters (or Hanja) that are associated with 상, so keep in mind that not all of the words that have 상 in them are related.

The word 상 (上) is related to "up", "high", or "on".

상 (high) + 하 (low) = 상하 上下 = above and below; 1st and 2nd volumes of a book

상 (up) + 경 (Seoul) = 상경 上京 = going (up) to the capital city, Seoul, from another area in Korea

상 (high) + 위 (rank, position) = 상위 上位 = high rank

> Related Vocabulary
>
> 위치 位置 = location
>
> 상위권 上位圈 = high ranking group

상 (high) + 반 (half) + 기 (period) = 상반기 上半期 = first half of the year

> Related Vocabulary
>
> 하반기 下半期 = second half of the year

Track 43

상 (high) + 사 (be in charge) = 상사 上司 = (one's) boss; superior

상 (up) + 장 (market, yard) = 상장 上場 = go public and be listed on the stock market

> Related Vocabulary
>
> 상장되다 上場-- = to be listed on the stock market
>
> 상장하다 上場-- = to go public on the market
>
> 상장* 賞狀 = certificate of award   * You pronounce this one as [상짱].

상 (high) + 급 (grade) = 상급 上級 = advanced; higher level

> Related Vocabulary
>
> 상급반 上級班 = higher class; advanced class

상 (up) ＋ 공 (empty, air) ＝ 상공 上空 ＝ sky (above a certain place)

* This is never used alone.

Ex)

서울 상공 -- 上空 ＝ the sky in Seoul

상 (up) ＋ 승 (go up) ＝ 상승 上昇 ＝ increase; rise; climb

Ex)

물가 상승 物價 上昇 ＝ rise in prices

물가가 상승하다 ＝ product prices go up

Related Vocabulary

승강기 昇降機 ＝ elevator

상 (high) ＋ 류 (flow) ＝ 상류 上流 ＝ upper class; upper region of a river

Related Vocabulary

상류층 上流層 ＝ upper class (socio-economic status)

북 (north) ＋ 상 (go up) ＝ 북상 北上 ＝ moving north (e.g. typhoon)

* This is used more when talking about weather, like a storm or typhoon, not about people.
You will hear it in a weather forecast.

Related Vocabulary

일기 예보 日氣 豫報 ＝ weather forecast

사 (history) ＋ 상 (on) ＝ 사상 史上 ＝ in history; all-time

Ex)

사상 최대 史上 最大 = the biggest of all time

업무 (work) + 상 (on) = 업무상 業務上 = for work; for business

Ex)

업무상 메일 業務上 -- = business e-mail

업무상 전화 業務上 電話 = business call

업무상 제주도에 갔어요. = I/He/She went to Jeju Island for work.

조 (grandfather) + 상 (high) = 조상 祖上 = ancestor

상 (up) + 의 (clothes) = 상의 上衣 = (clothes) tops

Track
43

Related Vocabulary

하의 下衣 = (clothes) bottoms

정 (top) + 상 (on) = 정상 頂上 = top; summit

세 (humanity) + 상 (on) = 세상 世上 = world

Related Vocabulary

세계 世界 = world

옥 (house) + 상 (on) = 옥상 屋上 = rooftop

Tense Structures, and Situational Expressions

Sample Dialogue

Track
44

주연: 그거 들었어요? 최경은 선수가 세계
랭킹 1위래요.

예지: 우와! 우리나라 피겨 선수가
세계 정상에 오른 건 사상 처음
아니에요?

주연: 맞아요. 상반기에 부상으로 쉬어서
걱정했는데, 진짜 대단한 것 같아요.

*Jooyeon: Did you hear that Kyeong-eun Choi ranked
first in the world?*

*Yeji: Wow! Isn't this the first time in history a Korean
figure skater has topped the world rankings?*

*Jooyeon: That's correct. I was worried because she
was injured and had to rest for the first half of
the year. She's so amazing.*

✎ Exercises for Lesson **22**

Fill in the blanks with the appropriate Sino-Korean word from the lesson.

1. The key word element $\Big($ $\Big)$ is related to "up", "high", or "on".

2. $\Big($ $\Big)$ = above and below; 1st and 2nd volumes of a book

3. $\Big($ $\Big)$ = increase; rise; climb

4. $\Big($ $\Big)$ = top; summit

5. $\Big($ $\Big)$ = world

6. $\Big($ $\Big)$ = rooftop

Check the answers on **P. 210**

153

LESSON **23**

Advanced Situational Expressions 3

> ## 제안할 때
> ### (Making Suggestions in Korean)

Track
45

Welcome to another lesson in the Advanced Situational Expressions series. Throughout this series, we will take a look at common situations and some of the advanced expressions you can use in each of them. In this lesson, we will introduce various expressions you can use when you want to make suggestions and proposals.

Sentence Structures

1.

How about doing...?

= Verb stem + -(으)(시)는 건 어떨까요?

= Verb stem + -(으)(시)는 건 어때요?

* "어떨까요?" is a little more formal.

    Ex)

    How about doing it this way?

= 이렇게 하시는 건 어때요?

= 이렇게 해 보시는 건 어때요?

= 이렇게 해 보시는 건 어떨까요?

2.

Why don't we do...?

= -(으)(시)ㄹ래요?

= -(으)(시)겠어요?

Ex)

Why don't we go to the meeting together?

= 회의에 같이 가실래요?

= 회의에 같이 가시겠어요?

Track
45

3.

I think it will be better to...

= -(시)는 게 좋을 것 같아요.

Ex)

I think it will be better for you to research more about this.

= 좀 더 알아보시는 게 좋을 것 같아요.

4.

I am thinking of -ing. What do you think?

= -(으)ㄹ까 하는데, 어떻게 생각하세요?

= -(으)ㄹ까 하는데, 어떠세요?

155

Tense Structures, and Situational Expressions

Ex)

I am thinking of moving the office (to another location). What do you think?

= 사무실을 옮길까 하는데, 어떻게 생각하세요?

Fixed Expressions

1.

차라리

= It would rather be...

= It will be more... if you...

Track 45

Ex)

차라리 안 하는 게 좋을 것 같아요.

= I think it would rather be better not to do it.

차라리 다른 제품을 쓰는 게 좋을 것 같아요.

= It will be better to use a different product (rather than sticking with the current one).

2.

아니면

= or

= or perhaps

= or if you do not like that option

Ex)

아니면 그냥 이렇게 할까요? = Or shall we just do it this way?

아니면 더 큰 장소를 찾아볼까요? = Or perhaps we should look for a bigger place?

3.

그러면

= if so

= if that is the case

= then

Ex)

그러면 행사를 연기할까요? = Then shall we postpone the event?

그러면 제가 해 보면 어떨까요? = Then how about me giving it a try?

4.

한번 이렇게 해 보는 것도 나쁘지는 않을 것 같은데요.

= It would not hurt to try doing it this way (just for this once).

* You could say, "한번 이렇게 해 보세요" but using the other phrase makes it a bit more polite.

Track 45

5.

일단 한번 이렇게 해 보는 거 어떨까요?

= For now, how about we try doing it this way?

6.

이런 방법도 있지 않을까요?

= Perhaps we can do it like this?

7.

저한테 좋은 생각이 있습니다.

= I have a good idea.

* Of course, ending the sentence with 있습니다 makes it sound formal, so if you speak in a less formal situation, you can end with 있어요.

8.

좋은 생각이 떠올랐어요.

= A good idea just occurred to me.

* 떠오르다 = to float up

9.

제안드리고 싶은 게 있습니다.

= I have a suggestion that I would like to make to you.

* 제안 = suggestion

** 제안하다 = to make a suggestion

*** 제안드리다 = (honorific) to give a suggestion

10.

이렇게 해 볼 수도 있을 것 같아요.

= I think we could do it like this.

11.

혹시 이렇게도 해 보셨어요?

= Have you, by any chance, tried doing it like this, too?

12.

이런 식으로 해 보는 것도 괜찮을 것 같아요.

= I think it will be cool to try doing it like this too.

* You could also give your suggestion first and add "-는 것도 괜찮을 것 같아요" after the verb stem.

Ex)

지금은 이렇게 하는 것도 괜찮을 것 같아요.

= I think it will be cool to do it this way for now.

지금 시작하는 것도 괜찮을 것 같아요.

= I think it will be cool to start now.

다른 사람이 해 보는 것도 괜찮을 것 같아요.

= I think it will be cool to try letting another person do it.

Track 45

Sample Dialogue

Track 46

경화: 요즘 운동을 시작해 볼까 생각 중이에요.

주연: 어떤 운동이요?

경화: 수영을 해 볼까 하는데, 어떻게 생각하세요?

주연: 복싱을 해 보는 건 어때요? 제가 해 봤는데 너무 좋더라고요. 체육관이 여기서 가까우니까 일단 한번 해 보고 결정하는 것도 괜찮을 것 같아요.

Kyung-hwa: These days, I am thinking I might start exercising.

Jooyeon: What kind of exercise?

Kyung-hwa: I'm thinking of swimming. What do you think?

Jooyeon: What about boxing? I tried it and I loved it. The gym is really close to here so it would be a great idea to give it a try and then decide.

✎ Exercises for Lesson 23

Translate each sentence into Korean using the expressions from the lesson.

1. How about doing it this way?

....

2. It will be better to use a different product (rather than sticking with the current one).

....

3. Or shall we just do it this way?

....

4. I think we could do it like this.

....

5. I am thinking of moving the office (to another location). What do you think?

....

Check the answers on **p. 210**

161

Tense Structures, and Situational Expressions

LESSON 24

It is just that…, I only…

-(으)ㄹ 따름이다

In this lesson, we will take a look at how to use the sentence ending -(으)ㄹ 따름이다. This is used to express the meaning of "only", as in "we can only…" or "what I did is just…". This is a somewhat formal ending and can be found in many official (usually apologetic) statements as well as contexts where the speaker is expressing hope or regret, such as "I only did what he told me, but…" or, "We can only wait for the result now."

Track 47

Conjugation

Present/Future Tense:

Verb stem + -(으)ㄹ 따름이다

Past Tense:

Verb stem + -았/었/였- + -(으)ㄹ 따름이다

Ex)

기다리다 (= to wait)

→ 기다리 + -(으)ㄹ 따름이다

→ 기다릴 따름입니다. (= I can only wait.)

말해 주다 (= to tell someone)

→ 말해 주 + -었- + -(으)ㄹ 따름이다

→ 말해 줬을 따름입니다. (= I did nothing but tell them about it.)

Sample Sentences

부끄러울 따름입니다.

= I am just ashamed of it/my mistake/what I did/what happened.

(I have nothing else to say; I cannot say anything but this; I cannot think of anything else

but this.)

Track
47

제가 이 상을 받을 수 있게 도와주신 모든 분들께* 감사할 따름입니다.

= I am just grateful to everybody who helped me receive this award.

* -께 is an honorific version of -에게.

정말 놀라울 따름입니다.

= All I can say is that I am surprised.

= It is really shocking. That is all I can say.

* You might hear someone say this while watching someone do something really

amazing at an event.

저는 해야 할 일을 했을 따름입니다.

= I just did what I had to do.

이런 일이 생겨서, 저희는 정말 당황스러울 따름입니다.

= We are just really baffled that something like this happened.

Difference between 따름입니다 and 뿐입니다

뿐입니다 also has the same meaning, but 뿐입니다 is commonly used in spoken Korean and in a lighter, less formal setting. For example, "저는 해야 할 일을 했을 따름입니다" can be changed to "저는 해야 할 일을 했을 뿐이에요" to be less formal.

Track 47

Sample Dialogue

Track 48

진행자 1: 저희 방송이 곧 10주년을 맞이합니다!

진행자 2: 우와! 이 프로그램을 처음 시작한 게 엊그제 같은데 벌써 10년이 지났다니 놀라울 따름이네요.

진행자 1: 맞아요. 이렇게 오랫동안 사랑해 주신 시청자 여러분께 감사할 따름이죠.

진행자 2: 시청자 여러분들의 사랑에 보답할 수 있도록 저희는 앞으로도 최선을 다하겠습니다.

MC1: The 10th anniversary of our TV program is around the corner!

MC2: Wow! All I can say is it's surprising that it has already been almost 10 years since this program was first aired, which feels like just yesterday to me.

MC1: Right. We are just so grateful to all the viewers who have given a lot of support to this show for so long.

MC2: We promise you that we will keep doing our best to reciprocate your support.

165

✏ *Exercises for Lesson* **24**

Fill in the blanks using -*(으)ㄹ* 따름입니다.

1. I can only wait.

= ( ).

2. I am just ashamed of it/what I did/what happened.

= ( ).

3. I just did what I had to do.

= 저는 해야 할 일을 ( ).

4. We are just really baffled that something like this happened.

= 이런 일이 생겨서, 저희는 정말 ( ).

5. I am just grateful to everybody who helped me receive this award.

= 제가 이 상을 받을 수 있게 도와주신 모든 분들께 ( ).

Check the answers on **P. 210**

LESSON **25**

Advanced Situational Expressions 4

부정할 때
(Defending in Korean)

Welcome to another lesson in the Advanced Situational Expressions series. Throughout this series, we will take a look at common situations and some of the advanced expressions you can use in each of them. In this lesson, we will introduce various expressions you can use when you want to defend, deny, or negate something.

Track
49

1.

그렇지 않아요.

= That is not true.

= That is not how it is.

= It is not like that.

2.

그게 아니고요.

= That is not true.

= That is not how it is.

= No, I am not talking about that.

167

= That is not the issue here.

* Sometimes in casual speech, people might say, "그게 아니구요" That is fine while speaking, but when writing, you should write, "아니고요."

3.

그건 아닌 것 같아요.

= I do not think that is how it is.

= I do not think it is true.

= I do not think that is the case.

* You can also say, "그건 아닌 것 같은데요."

4.

아니요, 제 말은 그게 아니고요.

= No, that is not what I am saying.

= No, that is not what I mean.

Track
49

5.

절대 그럴 리가 없어요.

= That is impossible.

= That cannot be true.

6.

말도 안 돼요.

= It does not even make sense.

= That is not even possible.

* This one is often used when you are shocked or surprised.

7.

그런 뜻으로 한 말이 아니에요.

= I did not mean what I said.

= What I said does not mean that.

8.

뭔가 잘못 아셨을 거예요.

= You must be mistaken about something.

9.

분명 뭔가 오해가 있는 것 같아요.

= I am sure there is a misunderstanding.

= There must be a misunderstanding.

Track 49

10.

꼭 그런 건 아니고요.

= It is not exactly like that.

11.

그렇다고 보기는 힘들죠.

= It is hard to say that is the case.

= You cannot really say it is.

12.

아직 확실히 정해진 건 아니에요.

= It is not decided for sure yet.

= It is not final yet.

Sample Dialogue

Track 50

석진: 현우 씨가 저를 굉장히 싫어하는 것 같아요.

캐시: 네? 말도 안 돼요. 절대 그럴 리가 없어요. 왜 그렇게 생각해요?

석진: 현우 씨가 제 전화만 안 받는 것 같아서요.

캐시: 그건 아닌 것 같아요. 제 전화도 항상 안 받거든요.

Seokjin: I think Hyunwoo really hates me.

Cassie: What? No way. That can't be true. What made you think that?

Seokjin: He never answers my calls.

Cassie: I don't think that's the case. He never answers my calls, either.

🖊 Exercises for Lesson 25

Choose the answer that is NOT an appropriate response.

Check the answers on **p.210**

1.

A: Do you think he dislikes me?

B: ....

① 그건 아닌 것 같아요.
② 절대 그럴 리가 없어요.
③ 잘돼서 정말 다행이에요.

2.

A: I heard she is going to quit her job very soon.

B: ....

① 지금은 생각이 없어요.
② 말도 안 돼요.
③ 분명 뭔가 오해가 있는 것 같아요.

3.

A: You mean this is all my fault?

B: ....

① 제 말은 그게 아니고요.
② 그런 뜻으로 한 말이 아니에요.
③ 저는 괜찮습니다.

4.

A: Is this the only way to boost our sales?

B: ....

① 꼭 그런 건 아니고요.
② 잘됐을 거예요.
③ 그렇지 않아요.

5.

A: So, is it the price that holds us back?

B: ....

① 그렇다고 보기는 힘들죠.
② 꼭 그런 건 아니고요.
③ 오늘 일이 잘 풀리는 것 같아요.

LESSON **26**

Advanced Idiomatic Expressions 5

몸 (Body)

Track 51

This is an Advanced Idiomatic Expressions lesson related to 몸, the body. In order to fully understand and use the expressions introduced in this series, it is essential that you understand the grammatical structure of the sentences. When you come across a grammar point with which you are unfamiliar, please go back and review the related lessons.

Keyword: **몸** = body

I. **몸이 약하다** = to be weak

The verb 약하다 itself already means "to be weak", but if you say that someone is 약해요, it means that he/she is in a weak position or his/her athletic ability or skill is not superior, rather than his/her body is weak. A similar expression is 몸이 허약하다.

Ex)

저는 어렸을 때 몸이 약했어요.

= When I was small, I was a weak child.

* If you just say, "저는 어렸을 때 약했어요", people might think you were weak not just physically, but spiritually and mentally, too.

2. 몸이 튼튼하다 = to be strong; to be healthy

튼튼하다 can be used for many things - furniture, teeth, car, and so on. Therefore, when you want to specify that someone has a robust or healthy body, you need to use the word 몸 together with 튼튼하다.

Ex)

저는 몸이 튼튼해서 감기에 잘 안 걸려요.

= I am healthy/strong so I do not catch colds easily.

Track 51

* Keep in mind that the opposite of 약하다 is 강하다, but in this case you would not use 강하다. Instead, you should use 튼튼하다.

3. 몸이 근질거리다 = to be anxious/raring to do something
▷ 근질거리다 = to be itchy

When you are itching to do something, it means that you have not done something that you have wanted to do for a long time and cannot wait to do it, or that you are anxiously looking forward to starting something. You can use the expression 몸이 근질거리다 to express how much you want to start moving and get rid of the itch.

Ex)

요즘에 운동을 안 했더니 몸이 근질거려요.

= I have not done any exercise recently, so I am dying to start working out again.

173

4. 몸이 좋다/안 좋다 = to be in good shape/to be not healthy; to not feel well

When you say 몸이 좋다, it means that someone is in good shape or very fit and well-built. When you say the opposite, 몸이 안 좋다, it does not mean that the person is not fit; it means that the person is not feeling well.

Ex)
몸이 안 좋을 때에는 충분히 자는 게 좋아요.
= When you are not feeling well, you need to get enough sleep.

5. 몸을 만들다 = to build up one's body; to work out to get fit

Track 51

You cannot "make" a body, but in Korean, if you say 몸을 만들다, it means "to build up" one's body or to build muscles. It can also mean "to lose weight to get fit" in some contexts. If you want to specifically say "to build up muscles", you can use the phrase 근육을 만들다.

Ex)
요즘 몸 만들려고 운동을 열심히 하고 있어요.
= These days I am working out hard in order to get fit/build muscles.

6. 몸을 사리다 = to spare oneself; to be cautious and not take any risk

몸을 사리다 means to play it safe and keep away from possible risks. It can be used both with positive and negative connotations.

Ex)

저 운동선수는 몸을 안 사리고 위험한 기술을 많이 시도해서, 많이 다쳤어요.

= That athlete has tried many dangerous techniques without worrying about his safety, so he has gotten hurt many times.

7. 몸에 배다 = to become a habit; to get comfortable doing something repeatedly

배다 originally means that a color or smell is stained or saturated on clothes or in places, but when a behavior or skill is saturated into your body, it means that it has become a habit or you have grown so used to it that you can do it without effort.

Track 51

Ex)

처음에는 어색했는데 벌써 몸에 뱄어요.

= It was unfamiliar and awkward at first, but I have grown used to it.

8. 몸을 혹사시키다 = to overexert oneself; to overwork

When you overwork yourself or do not get enough rest, what you are doing is "exploiting" or "overexerting" your body. In Korean, you say 몸을 혹사시키다 instead of 자신(oneself)을 혹사시키다. If you want to emphasize "yourself", you can add the word 자기 and say 자기 몸을 혹사시키다.

Ex)

왜 그렇게 자기 몸을 혹사시켜요? 쉬면서 하세요.

= Why do you overwork yourself? Get some rest from time to time.

175

9. **몸을 망치다** = to ruin one's health

망치다 means to screw something up. Therefore, when you say **몸을 망치다**, it means to ruin one's health, usually by drinking too much, not sleeping enough, or working too much.

Ex)

아무리 젊어도, 잠을 안 자고 공부하면 몸을 망쳐요.

= No matter how young you are, if you only study without sleeping, you will ruin your health.

Track 51

Sample Dialogue

Track 52

정우: 민성 씨는 몸이 약한데 왜 그렇게
　　 운동을 심하게 해요?

민성: 몸이 약하니까 몸을 튼튼하게 만들기
　　 위해서 하죠. 그리고 운동하는 김에
　　 몸도 만들고 싶어서요.

정우: 그래도 그렇게 몸을 혹사시키는 건
　　 좋지 않아요. 오히려 몸을 망치는
　　 지름길이에요.

민성: 정말요?

정우: 네. 조금 몸을 사릴 필요가 있을 것
　　 같아요.

Jeong-woo: Why do you always work out so much
　　　　　 even though your body is weak?

Minseong: Because I am weak, I work out so that
　　　　　 I can get stronger. While I am working
　　　　　 out, I also want to get fit.

Jeong-woo: But it's not good to overwork yourself
　　　　　 like that. You could wind up ruining
　　　　　 your health.

Minseong: Really?

Jeong-woo: Of course. I think you need to go easy
　　　　　 on your body.

177

Check the answers on **p.210**

✎ Exercises for Lesson **26**

Fill in the blanks with the appropriate idioms with 몸 *from the lesson.*

1. (   )

= to be anxious/raring to do something

2. (   )

= to be not healthy; to not feel well

3. (   )

= to become a habit; to get comfortable doing something repeatedly

4. (   )

= to ruin one's health

5. (   )

= to overexert oneself; to overwork

Improve Proficiency with Idiomatic Phrases,

LESSON **27**

Advanced Situational Expressions 5

칭찬할 때
(Complimenting in Korean)

Welcome to another lesson in the Advanced Situational Expressions series. Throughout this series, we will take a look at common situations and some of the advanced expressions you can use in each of them. In this lesson, we will introduce various expressions you can use when you want to make compliments about or to someone.

Track 53

1.

우와, 이거 어떻게 하셨어요?

= Wow. How did you do this?

2.

어떻게 이렇게 하셨어요?

= How did you do it like this?

= How did you do that?

= How were you able to do such a difficult thing?

3.

(정말) 잘 하신 거예요.

= You have done a good thing.

= You have made the right choice.

= It is a good thing you did that.

* You could simply say, "(정말) 잘 하셨어요" and in 반말, "(정말) 잘 했어."

4.

정말 잘하시네요.

= You are really good at it.

* You can say it more specifically by adding WHAT they are good at in the beginning, such as, "수영 정말 잘하시네요 (= You are really good at swimming)", "요리 정말 잘하시네요 (= You are really good at cooking)", "노래 정말 잘하시네요 (= You are really good at singing)", etc.

Track 53

5.

어떻게 그렇게 OO을/를 잘하세요?

= How are you so good at OO?

6.

정말 대단하신 것 같아요.

= I think you are amazing.

= You are really inspiring.

* 대단하다 can be translated into many things in English: amazing, awesome, inspiring, impressive.

** You could put #5 and #6 together, such as, "어떻게 그렇게 수영을 잘하세요? 정말 대단하신 것 같아요."

7.

오늘 패션 너무 멋져요.

= Your fashion looks awesome today.

8.

오늘 옷이 너무 예뻐요.

= I really like your outfit today.

= Your outfit looks very beautiful today.

9.

요즘 젊어지신 것 같아요.

= It seems like you have become younger recently.

= You look younger these days.

* This is a good phrase for those who are over middle-age because younger people tend to use another word to say "to look younger", which is 어려 보이다.

Track 53

10.

갈수록 예뻐지시는 것 같아요.

= I think you are becoming prettier and prettier.

= You are becoming prettier day by day.

11.

저도 OO 씨처럼 OO을/를 잘했으면 좋겠어요.

= I wish I were good at OO like you.

= I wish I could do OO as well as you do.

12.

너무 부러워요.

= I am so jealous.

13.

○○ 잘하신다고 이야기 많이 들었어요.

= I have frequently heard that you are good at OO.

= Many people have told me that you are good at OO.

14.

도대체* 못하는 게 뭐예요?

= Is there anything you cannot do?

* 도대체 = how on earth; what on earth

Track 53

Sample Dialogue

Track 54

알렉스: 잭슨 씨, 어떻게 그렇게 한국어를
　　　　잘하세요?

잭슨: 한국 문화를 좋아해서 자연스럽게
　　　언어도 공부했어요.

알렉스: 너무 부러워요. 혼자
　　　　공부하셨어요?

잭슨: 네. 제가 사는 동네에는 한국어
　　　가르치는 곳도 없고, 한국어
　　　공부하는 사람들도 거의 없거든요.

알렉스: 우와, 정말 대단하신 것 같아요.

Alex: Jackson, how are you so good at Korean?

Jackson: I love Korean culture, so I naturally just studied the language, too.

Alex: I am so jealous. Did you teach yourself?

Jackson: Yes, there is no place to learn Korean in my town, and also there are not many people studying Korean.

Alex: Wow! You are so amazing.

183

✎ Exercises for Lesson 27

Respond to the following questions in Korean using the expressions from the lesson. Write down all the expressions that are suitable for each situation.

1. How would you compliment your co-worker's outfit in Korean?

....

2. You were so impressed to see Kyeong-eun solving a Rubik's cube in only 30 seconds. In this situation, how would you compliment her?

....

3. You saw Hyunwoo dancing and found it fascinating. In this situation, how would you compliment him?

....

4. Seokjin brought some macarons he baked and they tasted heavenly. In this situation, how would you compliment him?

....

LESSON 28

Despite, Although

-에도 불구하고, -(으/느)ㄴ데도 불구하고

In this lesson, we will take a look at how to use the expression 불구하고, which means "despite", "in spite of", or "although". It is a rather formal expression and is more commonly used in formal settings, such as for business presentations and speeches, but it can also be found in some news reports, dramas, or movies.

Track 55

Conjugation

Noun:

Noun + -에도 불구하고 = despite + Noun

Action verbs:

Verb stem + -는데도 불구하고 = despite/although + Verb

Descriptive verbs (Adjectives in infinitive form):

Verb stem + -(으)ㄴ데도 불구하고 = despite/although + Verb

185

불구 is based on Chinese characters. 불 is "to not do something" and 구 is "to catch" or "to arrest someone". So, it means you are not caught or bound by the fact; you are a free soul.

Since 불구하고 is very formal, if you want to say the same thing in a less formal manner, you can just use the structure "Verb stem + -는데도" without adding 불구하고 at the end. This is only applicable to verbs.

Sample Sentences

경고에도 불구하고 전혀 달라진 것이 없어요.

= Despite the warning, nothing has changed at all.

(Less formal = 경고했는데도 전혀 달라진 게 없어요.)

Track
55

이미 충분히 설명을 했는데도 불구하고 아직도 모르겠다고 합니다.

= Despite having provided enough explanation, they say they still do not get it.

(Less formal = 이미 충분히 설명을 했는데도 아직도 모르겠대요.)

그 용의자는 증거가 있는데도 불구하고 무죄로 풀려났습니다.

= Although there was evidence, the suspect was declared innocent and was released.

(Less formal = 그 용의자는 증거가 있는데도 무죄로 풀려났어요.)

   * 용의자 = suspect, 증거 = evidence, 무죄로 = innocent, 풀려나다 = to be released

정부의 노력에도 불구하고 물가가 계속 상승하고 있습니다.

= Despite the government's efforts, prices are on a constant rise.

(Less formal = 정부가 노력을 하는데도 물가가 계속 오르고 있어요.)

숙면을 취했는데도 불구하고 계속 피곤하다면, 병원에 가 봐야 합니다.

= If you are still tired despite having had a good night's sleep, you need to go see a doctor.

(Less formal = 숙면을 취했는데도 계속 피곤하다면, 병원에 가 봐야 해요.)

　　* 숙면 = good night's sleep, 취하다 = to take

Track 55

Sample Dialogue

Track 56

주연: 경은 언니, 제니퍼 씨가 몸이 안 좋은데도 불구하고 여기까지 와 줬어요.

경은: 제니퍼 씨, 뒤늦게 초대했는데도 와 줘서 정말 고마워요. 몸은 괜찮아요?

제니퍼: 네, 괜찮아요. 초대해 주셔서 감사합니다.

경은: 아니에요. 제가 감사하죠. 맛있는 거 많이 먹고 재밌게 놀다 가요.

Jooyeon: Kyeong-eun, Jennifer has come all the way here even though she isn't feeling well.

Kyeong-eun: Jennifer, thank you so much for coming despite my belated invitation. Are you alright?

Jennifer: Yes, I am okay. Thanks for having me.

Kyeong-eun: My pleasure. Help yourself and I hope you have a lot of fun here.

✏ *Exercises for Lesson 28*

Fill in the blanks using -에도 불구하고 *or* -(으/느)ㄴ데도 불구하고.

1. despite the warning

= ( )

2. despite the government's efforts

= ( )

3. despite having provided enough explanation

= ( )

4. Although there was evidence, the suspect was declared innocent and was released.

= 그 용의자는 증거가 ( ) 무죄로 풀려났습니다.

5. If you are still tired despite having had a good night's sleep, you need to go see a doctor.

= 숙면을 ( ) 계속 피곤하다면, 병원에 가 봐야 합니다.

Check the answers on **p.211**

LESSON **29**

Advanced Situational Expressions 6

기분 좋을 때
(Expressing Happiness in Korean)

Track
57

Welcome to another lesson in the Advanced Situational Expressions series. Throughout this series, we will take a look at common situations and some of the advanced expressions you can use in each of them. In this lesson, we will introduce various expressions you can use when you feel very happy about something or a particular situation.

"To feel happy" is often translated as 행복하다 or 행복을 느끼다 in Korean, but you do not really use that to express feelings. 행복하다 is more about being happy in general or being a happy person in life. So, if you want to talk about everyday feelings, you can use the phrase 기분이 좋다 to say "to feel happy".

With that being said, since this is an advanced expressions lesson, we are going to skip basic phrases like 기뻐요, 기분 좋아요, etc.

I.

너무 신나요.

= I am so excited.

(Talking to oneself / Exclamation) 너무 신난다!

＝ I am so excited!

2.

진짜 너무 잘됐어요.

＝ I am so happy about it.

＝ I am so happy that you were able to do it.

* When you want to say that you are happy about the result of something that another person did, you can use this phrase. For example, if you were hoping that your friend got into the university of their choice, and he/she made it into that university, you could say this.

(Talking to oneself / Exclamation) 진짜 너무 잘됐다!

＝ That is good news! / That is great!

Track
57

3.

잘돼서 정말 다행이에요.

＝ I am so happy that it went well.

＝ I am so happy that the result is very good.

* When you say 다행이다, it has the connotation of you feeling relieved after having concerns that something might not go well.

4.

오늘 일이 잘 풀리는* 것 같아요.

＝ I think things are going well today.

* 풀리다 ＝ to be resolved; to be undone

5.

뭔가 좋은 예감*이 들어요.

＝ I have a good feeling about this.

191

* 예감 = feeling; hunch

6.

왠지 오늘 좋은 일이 생길 것 같아요.

= For some reason, I think something good will happen today.

7.

날아갈 것 같은 기분이에요.

= I feel like I am going to fly.

= I feel so happy that I feel like I can fly.

8.

너무 마음이 놓여요.

= I am so relieved.

= I am relieved to hear that.

Track 57

9.

이제 발 뻗고 잘 수 있을 것 같아요.

= I think I can finally sleep peacefully.

= I think I can finally sleep with my legs stretched out straight. (literal translation)

10.

이게 꿈인지 생시인지 모르겠어요.

= I do not know whether this is a dream or reality.

Sample Dialogue

Track 58

혜진: 지훈 씨, 취업했어요?

지훈: 네! 제일 가고 싶었던 회사에
　　　취업했어요. 이게 꿈인지 생시인지
　　　모르겠어요.

혜진: 정말요? 진짜 너무 잘됐다!

지훈: 감사해요. 정말 날아갈 것 같은
　　　기분이에요.

Hyejin: Jihoon, did you land a job?

*Jihoon: Yes! I got into the company which I wanted
the most. I don't know whether this is a
dream or reality.*

Hyejin: Really? I'm so glad to hear that.

*Jihoon: Thank you. I am so happy, I feel like I could
fly.*

193

✏ Exercises for Lesson 29

Check the answers on **p.211**

Write down how you would express your excitement and happiness in each situation using the expressions from the lesson.

1. You had a good dream last night so it feels like something good will happen.

....

2. You got straight A's and just saw your name on the Dean's list.

....

3. The results of your medical check-up came out and you turned out to be healthy. Now you are so relieved.

....

4. You are so happy to hear that your neighbor finally got a promotion.

....

5. You have a lot to get done by today and everything is going just as you planned.

....

LESSON **30**

Sentence Building Drill 14

Sentence Building Drill 14

Track 59

In this series, we focus on how you can use the grammatical rules and expressions that you have previously learned to train yourself to comfortably and flexibly make more Korean sentences.

We will start off with THREE key sentences, then practice changing different parts of these sentences so that you do not end up simply memorizing the same three sentences. We want you to be able to be as flexible as possible with the Korean sentences that you can make.

Key Sentence (1)
저는 들은 대로 전달했을 뿐이에요.

= I just told them what I had heard.

= I just delivered the message exactly as I heard it.

Key Sentence (2)
혼자 가지 말고, 친구들이랑 같이 가는 건 어때요?

= Rather than going there alone, how about going with your friends?

195

Key Sentence (3)

한 시간 후에 문을 닫는다고 하니까, 내일 다시 오는 게 좋을 것 같아요.

= Since they say they are going to close in one hour, we had better come back again tomorrow.

Expansion & Variation Practice with Key Sentence (1)

0. Original Sentence:

저는 들은 대로 전달했을 뿐이에요.

= I just delivered the message exactly as I heard it.

Track
59

1.

들은 대로 = just as I heard it

본 대로 = just as I saw it

읽은 대로 = just as I read it

아침에 둔 대로 = just the way I put it in the morning

제가 말한 대로 = just the way I said

2.

전달했을 뿐이에요. = I just delivered the message, that is it.

궁금했을 뿐이에요. = I was just curious.

잠깐 목소리를 듣고 싶었을 뿐이에요. = I just wanted to hear your voice for a little bit.

피곤해서 쉬고 싶었을 뿐이에요. = I was tired and just wanted to get some rest.

Expansion & Variation Practice with Key Sentence (2)

0. Original Sentence:

혼자 가지 말고, 친구들이랑 같이 가는 건 어때요?

= Rather than going there alone, how about going with your friends?

1.

혼자 가지 말고 = instead of going alone

여기에서 기다리지 말고 = instead of waiting here

걱정만 하지 말고 = instead of just worrying

직접 가서 사지 말고 = instead of going there yourself to buy it

위험하니까 직접 하지 말고 = since it is dangerous; instead of doing it yourself

Track
59

2.

친구들이랑 같이 가는 건 어때요? = How about going with your friends?

이렇게 하는 건 어때요? = How about doing it this way?

그냥 여기 있는 건 어때요? = How about just staying here?

인터넷으로 알아보는 건 어때요? = How about looking it up on the Internet?

Expansion & Variation Practice with Key Sentence (3)

0. Original Sentence:

한 시간 후에 문을 닫는다고 하니까, 내일 다시 오는 게 좋을 것 같아요.

= Since they say they are going to close in one hour, we had better come back again tomorrow.

1.

한 시간 후에 문을 닫는다고 하니까 = They say they are going to close in one hour, so…

여기가 제일 좋다고 하니까 = Since they say this is the best place

내일은 비가 온다고 하니까 = Since they say it is going to rain tomorrow

지금 질문을 받는다고 하니까 = They say they are receiving questions now, so…

2.

내일 다시 오는 게 좋을 것 같아요. = We had better come back again tomorrow.

이건 안 하는 게 좋을 것 같아요. = We had better not do this.

오늘은 좀 쉬는 게 좋을 것 같아요. = I had better get some rest today.

오늘은 일찍 자는 게 좋을 것 같아요. = I had better go to bed early today.

다음번엔 좀 일찍 시작하는 게 좋을 것 같아요. = We had better get started a little early next time.

Track 59

Sample Dialogue

Track
60

경화: 내일 엄청 추울 거라고 들었는데 왜
　　　야외에서 먹는 식당으로 예약했어요?

예지: 네? 저는 부장님이 하라는 대로 했을
　　　뿐이에요.

경화: 거기서 회식하지 말고 다른 곳에서 하는
　　　건 어때요?

예지: 저 말고 부장님한테 물어보세요.

경화: 부장님, 내일 엄청 춥다고 하니까
　　　실내에서 먹을 수 있는 식당으로
　　　예약하는 게 좋을 것 같아요.

*Kyung-hwa: I heard that it is going to be really
cold tomorrow. Why did you reserve an
outdoor restaurant?*

*Yeji: Huh? I just did what the director told me to
do.*

*Kyung-hwa: Rather than having the company
dinner there, why don't we have it
somewhere else?*

Yeji: Please ask the director, not me.

*Kyung-hwa: Sir, they say that it is going to be
really cold tomorrow, so I think we better
make reservations at a restaurant where we
can eat indoors.*

✐ Exercises for Lesson *30*

Find the best matching phrases and combine them into one sentence.

읽은 대로

걱정만 하지 말고

한 시간 후에 문을 닫는다고 하니까

내일 다시 오는 게 좋을 것 같아요.

전달했을 뿐이에요.

인터넷으로 알아보는 건 어때요?

Check the answers on **p.211**

1.

2.

3.

들은 대로

혼자 가지 말고

내일은 비가 온다고 하니까

친구들이랑 같이 가는 건 어때요?

이건 안 하는 게 좋을 것 같아요.

전달했을 뿐이에요.

4.

5.

6.

Jeju Batdam
(밭담/돌담)

In a blog in the Level 6 book, we talked about how Jeju Island is known for its abundance of rocks. Well, for any farmers out there, you know rocks are not that great for farming. So, what did the people of Jeju do to condition the land for farming? They dug up the soil! As you may know, Jeju was created by volcanoes, thus making most of the soil unsuitable for farming. Therefore, farmers had to go around plowing the ground and digging up the layer of volcanic soil. In doing so, they also got rid of the volcanic rocks or basalt that was also embedded in the soil.

Once they made the land suitable for farming, what were they going to do with all of these rocks they had lying around? One thing they did was to use the rocks to build walls around their fields. This is where we get batdam (밭담) or doldam (돌담) in Korean. Doldam means "stone wall". Farmers would use these black stones around their crop fields. One of the reasons they built these walls was due to the wind; Jeju's strong winds would carry away the soil and damage crops. Not only that, but any animals in the area could also come through and destroy the crops by eating them or stomping on them. However, with these walls, animals could no longer enter the fields and the wind would also be blocked. But not all of the wind.

If you look closely at the walls, you will notice gaps between the rocks. You might be wondering why they would include gaps in the rocks if they were trying to keep out the wind. It is actually quite smart as the holes in the walls allow the wind a path to escape, relieving some of the pressure that would otherwise build up if the holes did not exist. One person was quoted as saying, "People of Jeju accommodated the wind, rather than

conquered it." Due to this method, these walls have been able to withstand natural disasters for over a thousand years!

Not only have these walls been around for a long time, they are also quite long. If you added up the lengths of all of the walls, they would stretch out over 22,000 km (13,670 miles)! From above, these walls look impressive and have been given the nickname, "Black Dragon Great Wall" just to emphasize the seemingly endless black walls around Jeju Island.

Due to the importance of these walls, Jeju residents created a festival to celebrate them. One celebration is called, "The Batdam Festival" or "The Field Walls Festival". The year 2018 marked the fourth year for this celebration. While attending the festival, you can experience Jeju's unique farming culture during the nice breeze that autumn brings. You can also try out some delicious traditional food made with local ingredients. If you make a reservation, you can even receive a Donggoryang (동고량), a traditional lunch box. Those who make a reservation will also get other gifts as well which I am sure will make for a great souvenir to take back home. This traditional lunch box typically holds healthy foods like rice, vegetables, some meat, and fruit. The containers themselves are made with thin pieces of bamboo that were weaved together to make a rectangular basket.

The festival is held every year usually in September or October, and is held at the Jeju Batdam Theme Park in Woljeong-Ri. If you plan on visiting Jeju Island during this time, check out the festival and do not forget to make a reservation so you can get one of the lunch boxes and enjoy a nice lunch while learning about Jeju's unique farming culture!

Written by Johnny Bland

Level 8을 모두 끝냈어요*!*
축하합니다*!!*

ANSWERS

for Level 8, Lessons 1 ~ 30

Answers for Level 8, Lesson 1

1. 눈빛만 봐도 알 수 있다

2. 눈앞이 캄캄하다

3. 눈을 붙이다

4. 눈 밖에 나다

5. 눈썰미가 좋다

Answers for Level 8, Lesson 2

1. 눈 하나 깜짝하지 않다

2. 눈에 넣어도 아프지 않다

3. 눈이 멀다

4. 눈이 부시다

5. 눈에 띄다

Answers for Level 8, Lesson 3

1. 밥을 다 먹기가 무섭게/바쁘게

2. 공연이 끝나기가 무섭게/바쁘게

3. 문을 열기가 무섭게/바쁘게

4. 수업이 끝나기가 무섭게/바쁘게

5. 주문하기가 무섭게/바쁘게

Answers for Level 8, Lesson 4

1. 읽던

2. 친했던

3. 작았던

4. 지난주에 이야기하던 거예요.

5. 예전에 제가 자주 가던 곳이에요.

Answers for Level 8, Lesson 5

Possible answers:

1. 저는 괜찮습니다. / 지금은 배불러서 생각이 없어요. / 지금은 생각이 없어요.

2. 안 그러셔도 괜찮아요. / 안 그러셔도 괜찮습니다. / 저는 괜찮습니다.

3. 지금은 좀 곤란합니다. / 지금은 바빠서 안 될 것 같습니다. / 어려울 것 같습니다.

4. 됐어요. / 됐습니다.

5. 이러지 마세요. / 이러시면 안 됩니다. / 이러시면 곤란합니다.

Answers for Level 8, Lesson 6

1.

A: '완료'가 무슨 뜻이에요?

B: 끝났다는 뜻이에요.

2.

A: 안 가고 싶다는 말이에요?

B: 네. 안 가고 싶다는 말이에요.

3.

A: 갑자기 빨간불이 켜졌어요.

B: 정말요? 빨간불이 켜지면, 고장 났다는 뜻이에요.

4.

A: '휴업'이 무슨 뜻이에요?

B: 일을 안 한다는 뜻이에요.

Answers for Level 8, Lesson 7

1. 점 (點)

2. 장점 (長點)

3. 초점 (焦點)

4. 원점 (原點)

5. 요점 (要點)

Answers for Level 8, Lesson 8

1. 내일 사람들이 많이 왔으면 좋겠어요. (내일 사람들이 많이 오면 좋겠어요. is also possible.)

2. 제 선물, 마음에 들었으면 좋겠어요. (제 선물, 마음에 들면 좋겠어요. is also possible.)

3. 제가 스무 살이었으면 좋겠어요. (제가 스무 살이면 좋겠어요. is also possible.)

4. 내일도 날씨가 좋았으면 좋겠어요. (내일도 날씨가 좋으면 좋겠어요. is also possible.)

5. 주연 씨가 지각 안 했으면 좋겠어요. (주연 씨가 지각 안 하면 좋겠어요. is also possible.)

Answers for Level 8, Lesson 9

1. 아까 이야기한 책

2. (제가) 샀어요.

3. 중국어 배워 본 적 있어요?

4. 이거 읽어 봤어요?

5. 너무 무거워서 떨어뜨릴 뻔했어요.

6. 가끔 친구들을 만나고는 했어요.

Answers for Level 8, Lesson 10

1. 귀가 간지럽다

2. 귀먹다 or 귀가 먹다

3. 귀를 기울이다

4. 귀에 못이 박히도록 (듣다)

5. 귀가 얇다

6. 귀가 밝다

Answers for Level 8, Lesson 11

1. 어제 운동을 많이 한 데다가, 일도 늦게 끝나서

2. 물어봐야 알 것 같은데

3. 어차피 좀 기다려야 될 것 같아요.

4. 제가 어제 읽던 책인데, 어차피 다 못 읽을 것 같아요.

5. 일이 바쁜 데다가 감기에도 걸려서 눕기가 무섭게 잠들었어요.

Answers for Level 8, Lesson 12

1. 보고 싶어요. = I want to see. / I miss you.

2. 읽을 수 있어요. = I can read.

3. 가야 돼요. = I have to go.

4. 좋은 것 같아요. = I think it is good.

5. 늦을 수도 있어요. = I might be late. / They might be late.

6. 이상하지 않아요.

7. 지금 가요.

8. 저 착한 것 같아요.

Answers for Level 8, Lesson 13

1. 주 (主)

2. 주인공 (主人公)

3. 주부 (主婦)

4. 주장 (主張)

5. 주어 (主語)

6. 주도권 (主導權)

Answers for Level 8, Lesson 14

Possible answers:

1. 좋아요. / 좋습니다. / 네.

2. 당연하죠. / 물론이죠. / 네.

3. 네. / 당연하죠. / 네, 저도 그렇게 생각해요. / 네, 저도 같은 생각입니다. / 네, 찬성이에요. / 네, 찬성입니다.

4. 네. / 네, 맞아요.

5. 네. / 물론이죠. / 그럼요. / 안 될 거 없죠.

6. 네. / 좋아요. / 당연하죠. / 그럼요. / 좋은 생각이에요. / 안 될 거 없죠. / 찬성이에요.

Answers for Level 8, Lesson 15

1. 번역할 계획이에요. = I am planning to translate.

2. 안 갈지도 몰라요. = I might not go.

3. 일본어를 배울까 생각 중이에요. = I am thinking of learning Japanese.

4. 포스터가 떨어지려고 해요. = The poster is about to fall off.

5. 기다릴게요. or 기다릴 거예요.

6. 곧 도착할 것 같아요.

7. 집에 갈까 해요. or 집에 갈까 생각 중이에요.

8. 안 갈 수도 있어요. or 안 갈지도 몰라요.

Answers for Level 8, Lesson 16

1. 가슴이 두근거리다

2. 가슴이 답답하다

3. 가슴 깊이 후회하다

4. 가슴에 맺힌 한을 풀다

5. 가슴 깊이 뉘우치다

6. 가슴이 내려앉다

Answers for Level 8, Lesson 17

1. 이것만 아니면…

2. (그 사람이) 직장 상사만 아니면…

3. (그 사람이) 제 친구 친척만 아니면…

4. 공사 소리만 아니면 잘 잤을 거예요.

5. 오늘이 친구 생일만 아니면 그냥 집에 있었을 거예요.

Answers for Level 8, Lesson 18

1. 아는 대로

2. 도착하는 대로

3. 말한 대로

4. 하던 대로

5. 들은 대로

Answers for Level 8, Lesson 19

1. 나중에 후회하는 한이 있더라도

2. 다치는 한이 있더라도

3. 지는 한이 있더라도

4. 그만두는 한이 있더라도

5. 쓰러지는 한이 있더라도

6. 취소하는 한이 있더라도

Answers for Level 8, Lesson 20

1. 마음대로 하세요.

2. 아무리 바빠도

3. 아무리 비싸도

4. 사람들이 많이 왔으면 좋겠어요.

5. 집에 못 가는 한이 있더라도

Answers for Level 8, Lesson 21

1. 머리가 크다

2. 잔머리(를) 굴리다

3. 머리를 쓰다

4. 머리가 좋다

5. 머리를 스치다

Answers for Level 8, Lesson 22

1. 상 (上)

2. 상하 (上下)

3. 상승 (上昇)

4. 정상 (頂上)

5. 세상 (世上) or 세계 (世界)

6. 옥상 (屋上)

Answers for Level 8, Lesson 23

1. 이렇게 하시는 건 어때요? / 이렇게 해 보시는 건
어때요? / 이렇게 해 보시는 건 어떨까요?

2. 차라리 다른 제품을 쓰는 게 좋을 것 같아요.

3. 아니면 그냥 이렇게 할까요?

4. 이렇게 해 볼 수도 있을 것 같아요.

5. 사무실을 옮길까 하는데, 어떻게 생각하세요?

Answers for Level 8, Lesson 24

1. 기다릴 따름입니다.

2. 부끄러울 따름입니다.

3. 했을 따름입니다.

4. 당황스러울 따름입니다.

5. 감사할 따름입니다.

Answers for Level 8, Lesson 25

1. ③

2. ①

3. ③

4. ②

5. ③

Answers for Level 8, Lesson 26

1. 몸이 근질거리다

2. 몸이 안 좋다

3. 몸에 배다

4. 몸을 망치다

5. 몸을 혹사시키다

Answers for Level 8, Lesson 27

Possible answers:

1. 오늘 패션 너무 멋져요. / 오늘 옷이 너무 예뻐요.

2. 우와, 이거 어떻게 하셨어요? / 정말 잘하시네요. /
도대체 못하는 게 뭐예요?

3. 정말 잘하시네요. / 어떻게 그렇게 춤을 잘 추세요?
/ 저도 현우 씨처럼 춤을 잘 추면 좋겠어요. / 너무
부러워요. / 도대체 못하는 게 뭐예요?

4. 어떻게 이렇게 하셨어요? / 요리를 정말 잘하시네요. /
어떻게 그렇게 요리를 잘하세요? / 정말 대단하신 것
같아요. / 저도 석진 씨처럼 요리를 잘했으면 좋겠어요.

/ 요리 잘하신다고 이야기 많이 들었어요. / 도대체
못하는 게 뭐예요?

Answers for Level 8, Lesson 28

1. 경고에도 불구하고

2. 정부의 노력에도 불구하고

3. (이미) 충분히 설명을 했는데도 불구하고

4. 있는데도 불구하고

5. 취했는데도 불구하고

Answers for Level 8, Lesson 29

Possible answers:

1. 뭔가 좋은 예감이 들어요. / 왠지 오늘 좋은 일이
   생길 것 같아요.

2. 날아갈 것 같은 기분이에요. / 이게 꿈인지
   생시인지 모르겠어요.

3. 너무 마음이 놓여요. / 이제 발 뻗고 잘 수 있을 것
   같아요. / 다행이에요.

4. 진짜 너무 잘됐어요. (You could say "잘돼서 정말
   다행이에요" but it gives off the feeling that you or
   your neighbor have been worried if he/she might
   not get a promotion.)

5. 오늘 일이 잘 풀리는 것 같아요.

Answers for Level 8, Lesson 30

1. 읽은 대로 전달했을 뿐이에요.

2. 걱정만 하지 말고 인터넷으로 알아보는 건
   어때요?

3. 한 시간 후에 문을 닫는다고 하니까 내일 다시
   오는 게 좋을 것 같아요.

4. 들은 대로 전달했을 뿐이에요.

5. 혼자 가지 말고 친구들이랑 같이 가는 건 어때요?

6. 내일은 비가 온다고 하니까 이건 안 하는 게 좋을 것
   같아요.

MP3 audio files can be downloaded at https://talktomeinkorean.com/audio.